HAPPILY EVER AFTER
The Drew Barrymore Story

Also by Leah and Elina Furman
Published by Ballantine Books

THE HEAT IS ON: 98 DEGREES
HEART OF SOUL: THE LAURYN HILL STORY
ROCK YOUR WORLD: MEET THE MOFFATTS
IN HIS EYES: THE JULIO IGLESIAS JR. STORY

Books published by The Ballantine Publishing Group are available at quantity discounts on bulk purchases for premium, educational, fund-raising, and special sales use. For details, please call 1-800-733-3000.

HAPPILY EVER AFTER

The Drew Barrymore Story

Leah & Elina Furman

BALLANTINE BOOKS • NEW YORK

A Ballantine Book
Published by The Ballantine Publishing Group
Copyright © 2000 by Leah and Elina Furman

www.randomhouse.com/BB/

Library of Congress Catalog Card Number: 00-107182

ISBN 0-345-48325-1

Manufactured in the United States of America

INTRODUCTION

America's Angel

Our first meeting with Drew Barrymore took place when we were still in grade school. Although that was some eighteen years ago, we remember that day as clearly as if it were yesterday. We piled into the backseat of our parents' navy blue Buick Skylark and headed for the movie theater to see *E.T.—The Extra-Terrestrial*. Throughout the ride, all we could think about was the upcoming movie. We couldn't wait to get in our seats and see what all the kids in school had been talking about. At the time, we'd never heard the name "Drew Barrymore" before. We didn't know who she was, what she looked like, or where she came from. All we cared about was that lovable alien who'd made such an impression on us during TV commercials for *E.T.*

The two magical hours that we spent in the theater that Sunday afternoon surpassed our wildest expectations. As we stumbled out of our seats, trying to choke back the lumps in our throats and the tears in our eyes, we knew that for as long as we lived, we would never forget either E.T., or the pudgy little blond girl who almost stole the show.

Her name, of course, was Drew Barrymore.

While she might not have been the stuff of household conversation just yet, her face was permanently embedded in the mind of every man, woman, and child who'd seen Steven Spielberg's highest grossing movie to date, *E.T.*

Pretty soon, Drew was dubbed America's little darling and began popping up all over. When she starred in 1984's *Irreconcilable Differences,* we talked about going to see "the new Drew Barrymore movie." She was the first movie star with whom kids of a certain age could identify, the Shirley Temple of the 1980s, the cutest, the most famous, the best-loved kid in the U.S., perhaps the world.

President Reagan and the First Lady invited her to the White House. NBC put her front and center on the stage of *Saturday Night Live.* The Academy Awards and the Golden Globes saw her walking the red carpet year after year. Drew was always in the spotlight.

And then, just like that, she was gone. Not a snapshot, not a movie, not a word. Nothing.

In January 1989, she hadn't been out of circulation long enough for anyone to notice a conspicuous absence. That's when the *National Enquirer* sounded the alarm: E.T. STAR IN COCAINE AND BOOZE CLINIC—AT 13!

Parents were horrified. Kids of all ages were dumbfounded. "How could this have happened to our little Drew?"

The scion of the Barrymore acting dynasty, Drew was nothing less than a national treasure. For generations, the Barrymores had been making headlines on the stage, on the screen, and on the party circuit. Everyone knew of the illustrious family's personal woes, checkered with alcoholism and drug addiction. But Drew was supposed to be different. She'd spoken out against drug abuse. She'd starred in our favorite films. She'd captured our hearts as we watched her grow up. This wasn't supposed to happen to her.

As details of Drew's addiction began to leak out, the controversy wreaked havoc upon her image as a fun-loving but essentially down-to-earth child star. Overnight, Drew became the poster girl for excess and teenage rebellion. She went from everyone's role model to public enemy number one. Indeed, prevailing wisdom suddenly dictated that Drew Barrymore was nothing more than a *very* bad girl.

It was Drew's darkest hour. When she got out of rehab, no one wanted to hire her. Many of her old friends disappeared without a trace. Cast out of the industry, Drew might have easily reverted to her old habits. But just as all signs pointed to what might have been another tragic ending in the Barrymore saga, Drew chose to do the unpredictable—she fought back.

At fourteen years of age, Drew Barrymore authored *Little Girl Lost*, the autobiography that detailed her descent into and arduous climb out of the depths of despair. The book was an instant best-seller, and Drew was back on top, a heroine to young adults nationwide.

That was more than ten years ago. Over the last decade Drew has worked steadily toward reclaiming the very fame, fortune, and respect that she'd been so quick to throw away as a child. The 1990s have been good to Drew, and while this biography will recap some of the events narrated in *Little Girl Lost,* it is the new and triumphantly self-improved Drew who is the shining focus of *Happily Ever After: The Drew Barrymore Story.*

ONE

Heiress

Dynasty . . . the word alone conjures up a parade of grandiose images, which is perhaps why so much has been made of Drew Barrymore's legacy. Her genealogy bears the honorable Barrymore coat of arms; her dominion is the world of stage and screen; her crown jewels are gold-plated Oscars and acclaimed films. To earn this distinction, she had only to be born. Not unlike Prince William, Drew is the heir to a royal family throne. Indeed the Barrymores are called "The First Family of the Theater." Most of us naturally assumed that with this throne came a fortune.

Hearing of Drew's celebrated lineage, we believed she was born with the proverbial silver spoon. "Hollywood royalty," they said, and we envisioned her coming of age on a sprawling Bel Air estate where a staff of servants was paid to cater to her every childish whim. "Acting dynasty," they said, and we were led to understand that she was a princess and her life a fairy tale.

How were we to know the truth: Drew Barrymore was born into a single-parent household, a latch-key kid completely disconnected from the deceased ancestors who had so glorified her famous last name? "Drew and I started with nothing but the clothes on my back," Drew's mother, Jaid Barrymore, said on *This Evening with Judith Regan.*

No family. No friends. No money. How had it come to this?

Drew is the proud heiress of thoroughbred thespian bloodlines as pure as they are long. Reaching back into the 1800s, the glamour-personifying predecessors who informed Drew's talent were more than mere superstars. For over a century, the Barrymores have represented America's cultural aristocracy, that singularly charming, witty, and talented coterie that best exemplifies all that is most noble and most eccentric about true greatness.

It's mind-boggling to consider how many books, plays, and movies have been written to either spoof, honor, or expose the ostentatious display of genius that is the Barrymore family. Awards and theaters have been named after this hallowed clan. The story behind the family tree, however, is as full of corkscrew twists and hairpin turns as is the history of Drew Barrymore's public persona.

The young star's name is itself no flight of fancy, no last minute caprice on the part of her parents. In fact, every part of Drew Blythe Barrymore's auspicious moniker stems from a family surname. Drew is actually the maiden name of her great-grandmother Georgiana Drew, a renowned stage actress who was born in 1854 to the equally lauded actors John and Louisa Lane Drew of Philadelphia.

As the daughter of a celebrated husband-and-wife acting team, it is perhaps not surprising that Georgiana (or Georgie as she was more commonly known) went on to marry one of the most respected performers of her day, Maurice Barrymore. Born Herbert Blythe in 1847, Maurice came to the U.S. by way of Great Britain where he studied law at Cambridge. But donning the barrister's wig evidently failed to satisfy his flair for the dramatic; he quit the profession, changed his name, and joined the theater. By 1875 he was in New York.

It was while working as a leading man at Augustin Daly's theatrical company that Maurice met and fell in love with Georgie Drew. Within a year of his arrival in the U.S., the two were married. Countless rave reviews, six years, and three children later, the future of the Barrymore legacy was secured. Lionel, Ethel, and John Barrymore—never was so much raw acting talent assembled beneath one stage name. This is the triumvirate that would give the family its prominent place in performing arts history.

As the trio matured, so did their family's reputation. The upper crust of New York society was just as smitten with the Barrymores as the theatergoing Philadelphians had been with the Drews. Horse-drawn carriages, sparkling jewels, motley brocade gowns, everything was beautiful at the playhouse. On the home front, however, the Barrymore life lost some of its luster.

Beset by Maurice's infidelity and alcoholism, the Barrymore marriage was not a happy one. By far the biggest blow to the family, however, came while Lionel,

Ethel, and John were still in their teens. At only thirty-seven years of age, their mother died of tuberculosis, leaving her children to the care of their maternal grandmother, Louisa Lane Drew, who along with her late husband managed to endow the children with just as many vices as talents.

Like his kindred spirit of a son-in-law, John Drew had been known for his prodigious drinking. So severe was his condition that he actually reveled his way into an early grave long before either Lionel, Ethel, or John were even born. Meanwhile Louisa Lane, the grande dame of a matriarch whom the grandkids called Mummum and loved like a mother, rarely lost her icy reserve and preached the virtues of this stoicism by withholding both her approval and her affection from the children. These heirlooms from the Drew branch of the family tree would go on to characterize the Barrymores' lives, as tales of their infamous aversion to emotional entanglements and their fatal penchant for drugs and drink would subsequently snowball to monstrous proportions.

Strangely enough, these proclivities would endure to affect Drew Barrymore's life just as surely as if she herself had been born some one hundred years earlier into the Philadelphia home of her great-great-grandparents.

The saga of the three Barrymores is now the stuff of Hollywood legend. The Golden Age of American cinema wouldn't have been as bright had it not been for this troika of actors who rode the wave of filmmaking all the way from the silent screen to the talkies. Although today's generation of Barrymore fans might not know it, these were the Barrymores who made the real headlines and inspired awestruck mortals to pen so many documentaries, plays, books, and scripts.

Of the three, Drew's grandfather, John Barrymore, would emerge as the most admired actor of his age, while his elders, Lionel and Ethel, would go down in history as the Oscar-winning first siblings of stage and screen. Looked up to for their stunning good looks and eminent refinement as much as for their talent, the three third-generation actors made short work of becoming movie stars. Being the oldest, Lionel was the first to make his theatrical debut beside his illustrious uncle John Drew Jr. and his grandmother Louisa Lane. Despite her aspirations to a career as a concert pianist, Ethel was quick to follow suit. After jaunting off to England while still in her teens, she became the toast of the London stage, as well as the American girlfriend of one young Winston Churchill.

Although both Lionel and Ethel made the transition to films successfully enough, their triumphs paled in comparison to the nationwide idolatry inspired by John Barrymore's movie debut. Anointed "The Great Profile," John Barrymore became both a sex symbol and an artiste. For him, there would be no small or supporting roles. While his siblings ceaselessly toiled to efface their personas for the good of their characters, it was generally accepted that John was born a great actor. He *was* Hamlet, he *was* Richard III, and in the end, he *was* the American Laurence Olivier.

His salary was no small indication of his sway over the audience. When he starred with Greta Garbo in the

1932 classic *Grand Hotel,* John Barrymore's asking price was $150,000, and there was no shortage of takers who'd have spent even more for his services. In the eyes of the world, he could do no wrong. Whether he was berating members of the audience midperformance, drinking himself into oblivion at all hours of the night, or woefully neglecting his firstborn daughter, Diana Barrymore, John never lacked for either friends or admirers.

For all their personal problems, life for the Barrymores was a whirl of star-studded dinner parties, sparkling champagne toasts, mellifluous laughter, and scintillating conversation. Wherever they went, the flashing lights of cameras were sure to follow. They were the talk of the town, in any town that mattered. Widely loved and universally envied, the Barrymores always came out on top. In fact, for a very long time, the worst of their qualities seemed to be that no one could ever really find anything wrong with them.

Although John's star shone brighter than those of his tremendously successful and equally talented siblings, his alcoholism also proved to be a heavier burden. The compulsion for inebriation held all three Barrymores in a viselike grip. Lionel was a morphine addict, Ethel drank, and as for John, well, he never stopped drinking. As he himself once quipped, "There are lots of [acting] methods. Mine involves a lot of talent, a glass, and some cracked ice."

While work came easily to the screen icon, relationships did not. To cut a long and tragic story short, millions of squandered dollars, three ex-wives, and one widow later, the world mourned the death of John Barrymore, the most dissolute genius in Hollywood—while his four children struggled to come to terms with the mystery that was their father.

The year was 1942. John Drew Barrymore was ten years old. As the second and youngest progeny of John Barrymore's marriage to Dolores Costello, daughter of matinee idol Maurice Costello and a celebrated model-turned-actress in her own right, John took after his father's side of the family. He was all Barrymore.

Dolores's best efforts to keep her son from following in his father's self-destructive footsteps proved all in vain. This was despite the fact that he'd had hardly any contact with his wayward father since his parents' 1935 divorce. No sooner had John turned seventeen, than he defied his now-retired mother by quitting school for a life in the movies. For the son of "The Great Profile" and the "Goddess of the Silent Screen," as Dolores had once been known, the sky was the limit and Hollywood truly was the land of opportunity.

Of course, as the heir to his father's temperament, it was only a matter of time before John Drew Barrymore turned to drugs and alcohol. And the clock was ticking fast. John's first outbursts were the result of his inability to deal with authority. His behavior on the set of various plays was an affront to his stately aunt Ethel, who wanted nothing so much as to see her brother's son carry on the family name. Alas, it was not to be.

Although his performances in movies such as *The Sundowners* pegged him as a rising star, John's erratic and volatile behavior continued to wreak havoc upon his professional life. Even his marriage to Cara Williams and the birth of his son John Blythe Barrymore failed to slow down his drinking. Instead, John drank more than ever and faced legal problems, too. His arrests for everything from spousal abuse to drunk driving to hit-and-run accidents combined to wipe out any hope of a brilliant future in Hollywood.

Los Angeles in the Sixties was a paradise for the anti-establishment set, and John basked in his element, soaking up the marijuana, LSD, and free love as if these were the very marrow of the bone of life. There would be a divorce, a few small roles, and many more arrests before John met Ildiko Jaid, the woman who would be the mother of his daughter, Drew.

Ildiko Jaid wasn't much more than a Hollywood cliché when she first met John Drew Barrymore in the early 1970s. In other words, she was an attractive young woman in a waitress's uniform with big dreams of stardom.

Jaid had grown up as Ildyko Jaid Mako in Pennsylvania. Her parents' divorce had left her feeling angry and resentful. Yearning to lead the life that she saw on movie screens and in the pages of glossy magazines, the raven-haired beauty constantly defied her mother and left for Los Angeles as soon as she was of age. "I mean, there I was, stuck in Pennsylvania," she said in Drew Barrymore's autobiography *Little Girl Lost,* "and all I wanted was to go to Hollywood, be an actress, and hang out with rock stars."

Toward this end, Jaid tried her hand at modeling and acting. But in a town teeming with pretty young things much like herself, the lucrative jobs were few and far between. So, not unlike most struggling actresses, Jaid had to rely on waiting tables to eke out a meager living.

Working at the Troubadour, *the* live music venue of the era, made Jaid's less-than-glam job considerably more palatable. Every night brought with it a veritable cavalcade of the rock industry's best and brightest. "It was very cool then, the center of the L.A. music scene," Jaid recalled. "Jackson Browne played there, James Taylor, Elton John, The Doors. All those people played there in the early days."

Despite the years she spent immersed in this heady atmosphere, Jaid was as impressionable as a schoolgirl when she first laid eyes on John Drew Barrymore. His confident swagger and bohemian style immediately appealed to Jaid. All she could think was that he looked "very movie-starish."

When John first began to show interest in Jaid, she couldn't believe her luck. This man, who was some fifteen years her senior, seemed like the very personification of her wildest dreams. Plus, he was the owner of the most prestigious last name in Hollywood. Jaid knew that John would somehow fill her life with excitement, passion, and love. And for a long time, she truly felt as if she had indeed struck the mother lode of relationships.

"When I first met him he was *so* charismatic, I mean he could charm the skin off a snake, have the snake hand it to him and thank him for taking it off the snake's hands," she explained to Judith Regan. "He was so amazing at a time when the 'turn on, tune in, drop out generation' was very glamorous. He was the son of one of the most famous actors in history; he was incredibly talented; he was one of the smartest men I've ever met; he was so sexy that I practically trembled in his presence."

For all of John's boozing and drugging ways, Jaid continued to have faith in their future as a couple. To be sure, much of this complacency can be attributed to the "if it feels good, do it" spirit of the times. Practically everyone that Jaid came in contact with was either smoking pot, tripping on acid, or drinking till dawn.

Despite her boyfriend's advanced years, she never worried about the fact that his drug and alcohol abuse might be something more than a passing phase. The fact that all of his money had gone towards supporting his addictions also failed to sound an alarm. Instead, she focused on her crystals and the mystical nature of their connection, imagining that John was meant to be the father of her child. "I knew that he was the one with whom I was to have this child," she affirmed, "no matter what I had to go through—short of practically dying in the process."

Thus, after dating for nearly three years, the pair decided to get married. They moved their belongings into a small home in West Hollywood. But all too soon the honeymoon came to an abrupt end.

In his drug and alcohol induced haze, John would lash out at Jaid just as he had at everyone else who'd ever dared to love him. Of course, by this time, Jaid herself was hooked on John's presence. His violent outbursts did nothing to disuade her of the notion that they were meant to be together. It was a classic case of co-dependence—the worse John treated her, the harder she tried to change him back into the wonderful man she'd fallen in love with.

Still caught up in the web of the Barrymore mystique, Jaid could no sooner give up her dream of mothering a Barrymore than she could go back to Pennsylvania. So invested was she in the idea that upon learning of her pregnancy, she immediately decided to name the child Drew Blythe Barrymore. After all, what better way to symbolize the fateful union that had produced Lionel, Ethel, and John?

According to Jaid's recollections, if there was one person who wanted this baby even more than she, it had to be John. Sensing that his hold upon his wife was beginning to slip, he hoped that the baby would irrevocably bind them together. How then, did Drew wind up coming into the world with no one but her mother to raise her?

Ironically enough, the pregnancy that was meant to solder John and Jaid's marriage is what finally tore it apart. For all his good intentions, John was unable to turn his self-destructive streak around. The two fought constantly, but this time Jaid wasn't about to sit back and take the abuse. For the first time in her life, she was able to put aside her feelings of love for John and focus on the well-being of the baby that was growing within her. The self-examination left her with no choice. Since every day that she stayed with John posed a threat to her unborn child, she had to leave her husband, and fast.

The two were ensconced in a small room at the Tropicana Motel when Jaid decided to break the news. Much as she would have liked to spare him the pain, there was simply no way to soften the blow that her words delivered: "I'm leaving you."

John's response was one of complete and utter wrath. "He became so heartbroken and so furious and so angry because, he said 'I wanted this baby more than you and now this is what's taking you away from me,'" she said. "And he couldn't resolve the fact that he was losing me because of it . . . and I just saw something snap in him and he became completely like a wild animal and came to this decision that if he got rid of the baby that I would have to stay with him. . . . He started attacking me and I started screaming and hollering. . . . I rolled up in a ball and just tried to protect my unborn child."

That night, Drew Barrymore's life might have ended before it had even begun. But, as fortune would have it, someone heard Jaid's frantic cries for help and thought to call the police. When the cops arrived, John was still trying to beat his unborn child to death and Jaid recalled that "five policemen had to take him off of me."

If she'd had any second thoughts about leaving before, John's terrifying psychotic break convinced her—she and her baby were on their own. Sadly, taking matters into her own hands would not be as simple as all that.

Judging by his actions, it would seem that John had

taken complete leave of his senses. Not content with his actions at the Tropicana Motel, he went even further in his quest to strike back at the woman who'd broken his heart. When he realized that Jaid was leaving for good, he did everything in his power to ruin her life. "When I refused to go back with him," Jaid recalled, "he burned down the house, took all the assets, all the money, everything we had."

Without a dime to her famous last name, the mother-to-be had to work hard to make ends meet. She rented a small, albeit charming, one-bedroom apartment in a West Hollywood duplex and worked as an office clerk right up to February 15, 1975, at which point her coworkers realized that she'd better take a leave of absence or they were going to have an emergency on their hands. As a send-off, they gave Jaid a baby shower. It came not a moment too soon. Just one week later, on February 22, 1975, Drew was born.

When mother and child came home from the Brotman Memorial Hospital, there was no one to greet them at the door. They were completely alone.

TWO

Starlet

Three weeks . . . that was all the time Jaid had to devote to the pudgy, blond bundle of joy that was her daughter before the demands of everyday life pushed her back into the workforce. Now nearly thirty, Jaid found herself in the position of having to start from scratch—except this time, she had not one mouth to feed, but two.

For years, Jaid's life had revolved completely around John. This tunnel vision had effectively cut her off from the outside world. When Drew was born, Jaid couldn't even turn to her friends for support; she'd neglected them for so long. With her husband now completely out of the picture, Jaid had to bear all of the responsibility for little Drew. Her situation was desperate, but she was not the type to throw up her hands in defeat. Instead, she rolled up her sleeves and set to work.

Her first priority was a baby-sitter for Drew. Someone had to watch over the newborn while she looked for a job. As it turned out, getting work proved far simpler than finding good child care. Jaid was an expert waitress, and now that she had a daughter, a night job was just what the pediatrician ordered. Within a matter of weeks, her name was penciled into the waitress rotation at the hippest stand-up comedy club in town, The Comedy Store.

Somehow, the tips she made while serving drinks six nights of the week were enough to cover food and lodging, even enabling Jaid to relocate to a two-bedroom apartment that was just across the street. Jaid and Drew managed. Best of all, Jaid's job allowed her to spend plenty of quality time with Drew. "During the day I was with her," Jaid recalled, "but during the night I had to work."

In time, the single mom even managed to find affordable, if not the most dependable, baby-sitters—a family of girls who lived on the block. This stroke of luck allowed her to return to her first love, acting. She'd studied the craft for years, and badly wanted to steer her career back on track. That was, after all, the whole reason for her move to Hollywood all those years before.

Back in the swing of things, Jaid found that the audition circuit, coupled with her stage work, TV commercials, and Comedy Store gig, kept her very busy—too busy for a social life, and even too busy for Drew. Although it took her away from her daughter, work was the only way to pay the bills. In her heart of hearts, Jaid truly believed that she was doing it all for Drew.

Meanwhile, Drew was growing by the day. Eventually, she'd grow old enough to realize that most of her time was spent in the company of a baby-sitter, and that this was not necessarily the norm. While Jaid vehemently denies any such neglect, Drew has said that hers was the life of an "orphan" and that her "family life was no family life."

While Drew was still a toddler, Jaid had set a goal for herself: to be so successful that she could, in turn, give her daughter everything she'd always dreamed of for herself. Of course, the thing that Drew would come to want most of all was her mother's presence and attention.

The youngest Barrymore's career took flight at her very first audition. Yielding to the not-so-gentle prodding of a friend, Jaid took Drew to try out for a Gaines Puppy Choice TV commercial when she was eleven months old. Hundreds of babies, each the apple of his talent agent's eye, had turned out for the spot. The task sounded deceptively simple: babies would have to bond with a puppy as the camera crew looked on.

The high-pitched sound of bawling children pervaded the waiting room. But Drew was no crybaby. When her turn came, all could see that she took to the puppy right away. The feeling, however, was not mutual. Instead of licking or frolicking around Drew, the puppy surprised everyone by nipping her square on the nose. What was even more shocking, though, was Drew's reaction. Showing absolutely no fear in the face of a puppy bite, she broke into a hearty laugh. That was all it took. Drew was hired on the spot.

This small triumph represented Drew's tentative first step into showbiz. The fact is that Jaid remained unwilling to involve her daughter in the business at such a tender age. She knew full well that the cutthroat industry could cause irreparable damage to a child's fragile psyche. What's more, she couldn't very well squire her daughter around to casting offices when she herself had her hands full with her own auditions and work.

So, after Drew shot the commercial, her life went back to normal. With her mother gone so much of the time, who could blame the little girl for feeling disappointed and not a little bored? Soon, Drew wanted to get back into the act. The way she told it to *Interview* magazine, she was all of two years old when she first sat her mom down for a heart-to-heart.

"Acting is my dream," she began. "I don't want you to think that you're doing wrong by me by getting me an agent. I can't expect you to be sure about this, coming from a two-year-old, but please, this is all I want."

This little speech had been brought on by Drew's second acting experience. This time she played the part of a little boy in *Suddenly Love*, a made-for-TV movie starring *Laverne & Shirley*'s Cindy Williams. Her hair had to be cut short, but Drew couldn't have cared less. To her, all that mattered was that she was the center of attention. Adults were actually noticing her and praising her performance, and she felt exactly as if she was part of a family.

At the age of four, Drew finally managed to convince her mom to let her act. She'd summoned her every last ounce of eloquence and delivered a plea that made a lasting impression on Jaid. Furthermore, Drew had a well thought-out response for every one of her mom's arguments. Jaid couldn't believe her ears, "Four years old [and] so self-possessed," she marveled. "All of a sudden, the *Twilight Zone* music was coming in."

In light of the family history, Jaid might have thought

better of letting Drew have her way. But, what was the use? If her predecessors were indeed an indication, Drew was bound to get into the family business sooner or later. To keep her daughter from acting would only postpone the inevitable and, worse still, it would make Drew miserable. Seeing "all the Barrymore genes screaming out for recognition," she finally gave in.

The phone began ringing off the hook as soon as Drew began going out on auditions. In fact, Drew's new agent, J. J. Harris, had so much contact with Jaid and Drew that it seemed they'd not only gained an income but a family member. The cause of all this communication was, of course, Drew. Everyone loved her, and with good reason—charming her way into people's hearts was not a means to an end, but the pot of gold at the end of Drew's rainbow. She wasn't interested in the fame, nor did she particularly care about the financial rewards. More than anything in the world, she wanted to feel loved, and she knew just how to go about getting it.

As she watched Drew talking to casting directors, Jaid hardly recognized her own daughter. It was as if a whole new personality was coming out and taking over. No matter how bad a day the little girl had been having, she'd go from sullen and peevish to bright and outgoing in less than a second's time to impress the decision makers. In this way, Drew consistently beat out hundreds of kids, many of whom were much more experienced, to get all four of the first commercials she went out for. Neither her mom nor her agent had ever seen anything like it before. It was as if Drew had been born to act.

Spending so much of her time around adults, the precocious little girl quickly lost interest in kids her own age. Instead, she sought to fit in with the mother and father figures who surrounded her on the sets. Her own family was a complete mystery to her. She had yet to see any of their movies and knew nothing about their long line of accomplishments. To this day, Drew doesn't believe that her last name had any bearing on her string of early successes. "Even when I was four years old," she recalled, "people would be like, 'Oh, a Barrymore. They're trouble.' . . . It definitely didn't give me any advantages, but at the same time, I would never look at my family as a disadvantage."

To be sure, the innate stage presence and charisma that Drew's famous relations had so liberally bestowed upon her were hardly a drawback in the world of entertainment. In her personal life, however, these talents proved more a curse than a blessing. Working before she could walk, Drew grew up confused about her role in life. "I had a very different lifestyle," she said. "By the time I was three, I was a responsible employee-putting-dinner-on-the-table-type mentality, you know. I wasn't a kid. I was a living, functioning, breathing person in society."

As such, Drew behaved in a way that many thought was advanced for her young age. She read books by authors of the beat generation and listened to music of the psychedelic era. "I had a different childhood from anyone I knew," she attested. "I listened to Jim Morrison rather than *Sesame Street,* and I read Charles Bukowski. I thought that it was normal . . . It was just me and my mom. She didn't have many friends, and neither did I."

Who had time for friends? The Barrymore women were always on the go. If Drew wasn't auditioning, then she was working; if Jaid wasn't driving Drew to auditions, then she was either acting or waiting tables. Somewhere along the line, the mother-daughter relationship began to strain under the pressure. In fact, there were times when Drew felt so lonely that she sought out the companionship of the avocado tree that grew in her backyard. "I think it explains why I was a heavy child," she reasoned. "I ate so many avocados, like five a day. I sat outside with a spoon and a salt-shaker, and I was in purgatory when the avocados weren't ripe. I had a cheap swing set, and I would swing and eat the avocados. I hugged that tree every day."

There was, of course, a small array of relatives to keep Drew occupied. Her half brother, for one, would come by to baby-sit on occasion. Sometimes, her grandparents would drop in to visit from Pennsylvania. Even her father managed to show his face once in a rare while—although, the way he behaved towards Drew and her mother when he did come around often made them wish he wouldn't have bothered.

Drew's first memory of her father is foggy. She remembers waking up one morning to find a man standing in the doorway.

"Dad?" she said, praying that her instinct was correct.

"Yeah."

That response had been all it took to infuse the tyke with a burst of hope. "I felt so happy thinking he was going to be back in my life," she recalled. "But it never happened."

In fact, Drew's erratic run-ins with her father would take on an increasingly negative tone. One time, John simply came raging into the household unannounced, taking Jaid and Drew completely off guard. He was drunk and angry. But her father's disheveled state and the smell of tequila on his breath failed to register in Drew's young mind. "Daddy," she yelled, as if her wildest dream had just come true. What followed was no tearful reunion, no heartfelt apology, but a display of violence that would scar little Drew for life. John pushed Jaid to the floor, and when Drew tried to intervene, he threw her across the room. Fortunately, she landed on a full laundry basket. Physically, she was fine. Her emotional state, however, was another matter altogether.

For a long time, Drew denied her feelings of resentment and anger toward her father. Through watching TV and observing the lives of other neighborhood kids, Drew learned that most children had both a mom and a dad. "Well, I must be some kind of alien because I don't," she thought. But the little girl didn't want to be different. She wanted to have a two-parent family like everyone else at her preschool. She wanted it so badly that she couldn't even see the truth: John Barrymore simply didn't have it in him to be a parent, not to Drew, not to her two half sisters, Jessica and Blythe (whom she'd never met), and not to her half brother, John, whose attraction to heroin would eventually lead him down the same road as his father.

Believing that she could make her father like her if she tried really, really hard, Drew blamed herself for his abusive behavior. Her fear of abandonment impacted every aspect of her life, but nowhere was it more evident than in her work. It was this classic actor's folly—the desire to win everyone over—that landed Drew in TV commercial after TV movie, and soon had her well on her way to the big screen.

The start of what would be a long and unconventional career in feature films began appropriately enough with 1980s *Altered States,* a movie that would go on to become a cult classic. Directed by Ken Russell, the film starred William Hurt as Eddie Jessup, a researcher who experiments with the effects of hallucinogenic drugs. Drew was to play Margaret Jessup, one of Eddie's two daughters. But the role itself was not as remarkable as the way in which Drew had gone about winning it.

While auditioning, she'd been grouped with more than thirty girls. Each had been handpicked for her suitability to the role. The audition process itself was on the informal side. In a rather unorthodox move, Ken Russell had gathered all the girls and began speaking to the group. Eventually, he ended his monologue by asking a question. Drew was the only one of the bevy to offer a reply. A conversation between the lauded director and the child prodigy ensued, and the two hit it off like a house on fire. By the end of the interview, Drew Barrymore's name was the only one on the list.

Whether or not Drew's family history had anything to do with the director's wish to cast her in this psychedelic flick is uncertain, but there's no doubt that it was her performance at the audition that provided the clincher.

Further proof that it was the young actress who was

simply irresistible and not her colorful family tree came in the form of her next audition. This time, she was being evaluated by none other than Hollywood's favorite golden boy, director Steven Spielberg. Having secured his place in the power-hitter's hall of fame with *Jaws, Close Encounters of the Third Kind,* and *Raiders of the Lost Ark,* Spielberg was helping to cast *Poltergeist,* a supernatural thriller that he'd written himself. Simultaneously, he was deeply enmeshed in his directorial work on *E.T.—The Extra-Terrestrial,* a charming tale of a displaced alien who is adopted by a human boy.

Although both *Poltergeist* and *E.T.* called for a flaxen-haired little girl to carry the day, neither movie had managed to find this elusive sprite. Then Drew came bouncing in to audition for the role in *Poltergeist.* Out of a hundred girls, it was Drew who immediately caught Spielberg's rapt attention. At six years of age, she was all cheeks, and looking at her, Spielberg couldn't help but think of Gertie, the as-yet-unfilled baby sister character in his other movie.

The pluck that the child displayed in the casting office cast the final vote in her favor. She was an unbelievable ham, going on and on about how she wasn't really an actress but a rock star. Her band, she confided to Spielberg, was called the Purple People Eaters. For the director who, heretofore, had thought he'd seen it all, this was the final straw. "When Drew came in, she had the part the minute she stepped into the room," Spielberg recounted on the *E! True Hollywood Story,* "because she began to make up these stories that she was a punk rocker, she had a punk rock band, she was going on the road . . . she's six years old, she's telling me she's going to do a twenty-city tour in America with her punk rock band! And then she kept making up stories and . . . she just blew me away. I mean there was no second choice. Drew Barrymore was the first choice for this part."

Clearly, Drew was much more than just a cute pair of cheeks; the girl was pure personality. After telling Jaid as much, Spielberg arranged for Drew's second audition, this time for *E.T.*

You can just imagine the heady ride home enjoyed by Drew and Jaid Barrymore on that fateful day. Steven *the*-director-of-his-generation Spielberg, the man who single-handedly redefined the A-list, was actually smitten with young Drew. And that love was not unrequited. Although she was only six, Drew had already seen and loved *Close Encounters*. A huge Spielberg fan, she'd read the *E.T.* script with voracious interest and was intent on getting the part just right.

What more need be said of the outcome? Drew's scream was right on pitch, her facial expressions right on target, and her delivery right on cue. She had won the part and, in so doing, changed the course of her life forever.

In September 1981, instead of entering the first grade along with the rest of her fellow six-year-olds, Drew began her work on *E.T.* Although she was the youngest child on the set, her older costars accepted her as an equal. Drew worked hard to gain this entry into the grown-up world. Aside from her professional experience and the erudition that she acquired through her reading, she adopted a maturity that was well beyond her years by modeling herself after the title character of her favorite film, Stanley Kubrick's *Lolita*. "[Sue Lyon] was so fucking sexy in that movie," Drew explained. "Every little detail I totally grooved on. *Lolita* became, like, this idol thing, you know? I totally fell into it."

Still, the underage femme fatale wasn't all business all the time. While working with her adolescent costars, Henry Thomas and Robert MacNaughton, Drew was often drawn into their tomfoolery. According to Mac-Naughton, the trio would run around the set, wreak havoc on their skateboards, and "just raise as much hell on the set as we could." As for Steven Spielberg's influence, not only did he not disapprove of such antics, he encouraged them. Dee Wallace, the actress who played the kids' mother, recalled that on Halloween of '81, Spielberg came to the set dressed "as a Gypsy woman. It was hysterical. Behind the camera is the biggest director in Hollywood—with earrings dangling and a bandanna on his head."

No doubt, it was this childlike sense of fun and adventure that drew the littlest Barrymore to the director. Unlike so many of the adults she'd known in her life, Spielberg always had time for Drew and positively showered her with attention. Before every scene, he asked for her input; whenever she felt lost, he somehow managed to find her.

"He was the greatest teacher," Drew enthused. "He taught me how it's so rude to patronize kids. . . . He taught me that great balance of how to have fun, because kids do wanna have fun; you don't want them to grow up without having that."

By January 1982, the shoot was over and Steven Spielberg was Drew's unofficial godfather and mentor. To this day, his office wall boasts a picture that Drew had painted for him when she was only six.

The four-month production schedule had effectively barred Drew from going to day school. On the set, her educational needs had been provided for by tutors. She and the other kids spent three hours per day in these makeshift classes, and the rest of the time they got to play at being adults. Drew couldn't have been happier with this arrangement. In fact, when the time came for her to start attending school, she found that being a regular kid took a lot of getting used to.

Making matters worse was Jaid's acting career, which, thanks to Drew's $75,000 *E.T.* paycheck, was finally shifting into high gear. The overworked actress suddenly found that she had the freedom to cut back on the hours she spent sweating over a drink tray, and focus more of her energy on auditions. Before long, she'd scored her first feature film role. Playing a prostitute in *Night Shift*, a Ron Howard film that starred Michael Keaton, Shelley Long, and Henry Winkler, Jaid was on call eighteen hours of the day for almost three months' running.

Having just come off the supportive atmosphere of the *E.T.* set and seeing so little of her mom, Drew felt completely cut off from the world as she'd known it, almost as if she'd been left to fend for herself. This desperate state led the little girl to take an extreme measure. "She felt so neglected and abandoned that she actually called her father and wanted him to take care of her," Jaid recounted on *This Evening with Judith Regan.* "And that is when I decided to give up my career completely and focus on her."

From that point on, Drew became not only the center of Jaid's existence, but its circumference and everything in between. Taking on the role of her daughter's manager, she tried the best she could to give every last ounce of strength to developing Drew's career. It was a job that was about to get considerably more difficult.

Throughout the filming of *E.T.*, Spielberg had been known to rub his hands together and say, "This is going to be my little movie, my little classic." Just goes to show that even great visionaries can't always predict the future. Sure, Spielberg had the classic part right, but there wasn't going to be anything "little" about *E.T.— The Extra-Terrestrial.*

Even during the early test screenings, it was obvious that *E.T.* would defy all expectations. Audiences were laughing, crying, and even applauding in all the right places. When it was screened as an unofficial entry at the 1982 Cannes Film Festival, the sophisticated audience of industry insiders was said to have jumped to their feet for a standing ovation. In no time, all thoughts of a skimpy marketing campaign went right out the window as the Universal Pictures executives scurried to negotiate lucrative cross-promotional and licensing deals with fast-food franchises and candy manufacturers. Within a matter of weeks, *E.T.* was poised to be the blockbuster of the summer.

By now, most people know that as much money as *E.T.* was expected to make, it made that much more.

After its June 11, 1982 release, the movie stayed atop the charts for what seemed like forever. The extensive run eventually led to an astounding domestic box office gross of nearly four hundred million dollars (the fourth highest of all time). After the movie was released overseas, another three hundred million dollars plus was added to its worldwide gross. All told, the film turned into the type of phenomenon that spawns action figures, Halloween costumes, lunchboxes, pillow cases, and most important, a nation of rabid fans.

Considering the vastness and ardor of the film's fan base, it is perhaps not surprising that the most enduring symbol of *E.T.*'s success was, and is, the career of Drew Barrymore. The fame did not come gradually—with a TV appearance here, a magazine article there, and a bigger part down the line—but with all the velocity of a speeding train. Drew was quite literally an overnight sensation. The evening of the premiere, Drew was tucked away in a hotel room with her two child costars—it was to be her last night as a private citizen.

E.T. was something akin to Drew's initial public offering, and no sooner had the movie opened than her stock went skyrocketing into the stratosphere. Autograph seekers, photographers, curious passersby, all were hot on her trail, screaming her name, trying to ask questions, and always wanting something. "From the time I became famous in *E.T.*, my life got really weird," Drew explained. "One day I was a little girl, and the next day I was being mobbed by people who wanted me to sign my autograph or pose for pictures or who just wanted to touch me. It was frightening. I was this seven-year-old who was expected to be going on a mature twenty-nine."

Neither did the situation get any easier once the media got wind of Drew's identity—she wasn't just any Barrymore, she was *the* Barrymore. Now, inquiring minds wanted to know more than ever, and the entertainment press was only too happy to deliver news of Drew's every move. There was, of course, plenty of news to report. With *E.T.*'s unbelievably brisk business and rave reviews, the awards show invitations were not long in the coming. Drew was asked to the Oscars, the Golden Globes, the British Academy Awards, the People's Choice Awards, the Young Actors Awards, you name it, she was there. Even more immediate were Drew's promotional efforts on behalf of *E.T.* She sat beside Johnny Carson on *The Tonight Show,* flew all over the world for press junkets, and smiled pretty for the cameras of any magazine that wanted her on their pages.

Her highest profile invitation, however, had to be from *Saturday Night Live.* At seven years of age, Drew would go down in history as the youngest person to ever host this long-running program. Naturally, the days of rehearsal went by like a flash. In the context of a season that could well be termed the Summer of Drew, her time on the *SNL* set seemed like just another week of good times. She was the darling of the cast, palling around with Joe Piscopo, and laughing at the antics of Eddie Murphy. Having herself a ball, Drew was taken aback by the sudden arrival of the big night, the one that would require her to give a monologue on live television before a live studio audience.

Nervous and overwrought, the little girl confided her anxiety to the producers. Within a matter of minutes, a solution had been worked out. Instead of going through with the opening monologue, Drew would field questions from the audience. Breathing a lot easier, the consummate young professional got through the rest of the show without a hitch.

It's a fact: Drew charmed the pants off America. She became so much more than a one-hit wonder, she became a star, a prepubescent icon for kids and beyond.

The scripts began to pour into Jaid's in-box. She couldn't read them fast enough. One can easily imagine the scenes taking place behind the closed doors of studio executives' offices. If a writer came pitching a story idea that featured a young girl, it was almost certain that someone in the room would snap their fingers and say, "I got it. We can get that little girl, what's her name, Drew Barrymore, to do it."

As they say in Hollywood, Drew was hot. On the home front, however, Drew was anything but.

Drew had hoped that her work on *E.T.* would impress her distant father, but his reaction to her accomplishment was hardly that of a supportive parent. John's response to Drew's success showed him to be bitter and angry over his own failures. Referring to his daughter as a "so-called movie star," he ever so casually informed her that he had yet to see her movie.

John's blatant hostility opened the floodgates of Drew's repressed emotion. Unable to tolerate his hateful behavior any longer, she told him exactly what she thought of him in a mad rush of angry words, kicked a chair at him, and stormed out of the room determined to never see him again. At that point her feelings for her father were crystal clear: "I hated him while I was growing up," she said. "He was an abusive asshole."

Sadly, this show of bravado was just that, a show. Inside, Drew remained tormented by her father's demons. Meanwhile, her mom was acting more and more like a manager than a parent with each passing day. As the pile of scripts on Jaid's desk swelled to swamplike proportions, it seemed auditions and read-throughs came first.

Although she understood that her mom meant well, Drew couldn't help but feel deserted by the only two people in the world who were supposed to care for her unconditionally. Later on in life, she'd look back on her childhood and say, "I learned early on that family, as far as a mother and father, was not an option."

For her encore, Drew chose to star in the 1984 film *Irreconcilable Differences,* earning a reported $500,000. Although actors Ryan O'Neal and Shelley Long got top billing, the movie posters put Drew front and center, leaving no doubt as to who was the real star of the movie. "It felt very mature," Drew recalled. "I went from . . . a set of all kids to being the only kid . . . that was sort of when I started just getting into the responsibility and maturity and work life."

The film's plot revolved around the turbulent family life of Drew Barrymore's character Casey Brodsky. Seeking to obtain a divorce from her self-absorbed parents, a down-on-his-luck director played by O'Neal and a best-selling novelist played by Long, Casey drags them into court, wherein their story unfolds.

While the reviews were not often kind to the sentimental little picture—and, truth be told, the movie did not approach the grandiosity of *E.T.*—*Irreconcilable Differences* struck a chord with many of Drew's contemporaries. After all, who of us hasn't, at one time or another, wished to divorce, or at the very least trade in, one or both of our parents? Drew certainly had, as she so artfully demonstrated by her honest portrayal of Casey.

Delivering a strong performance on the set of this particular film, however, was more difficult than Drew made it look. In her autobiography, she recounted the constant bickering between the producer and the director, as well as their total disregard for her feelings and well-being, while crediting Ryan O'Neal as her guide and personal savior from the "utter hell" of *Irreconcilable Differences*. Drew wrote about one typical production scenario: "There was one particular shot—not even a scene, just a tiny shot—that involved me, and it took us somewhere in the neighborhood of forty takes before everyone involved was satisfied. By that point, I was so emotionally drained that I broke down and cried. I hadn't ever felt stress like that and no one even looked at me sympathetically."

After the film's three-month shooting schedule wrapped, the diminutive star was only too happy to take a well-deserved break from showbiz. With the money Drew had earned, mother and daughter were finally able to bid their West Hollywood bungalow a fond farewell. Their new digs was a two-bedroom ranch in the considerably less bohemian environs of Sherman Oaks. The Barrymores' days of living hand-to-mouth were finally at an end, and neither Drew nor her mom felt any compunction to return to work. In fact, Drew even considered giving up her career for good.

This dalliance with quitting the spotlight did not last long. With *Irreconcilable Differences* earning Drew a Golden Globe nomination for Best Supporting Actress and the influx of scripts showing no signs of slowing down, it was only a matter of time before America's favorite screen urchin was presented with an offer she couldn't refuse.

Enter *Firestarter*.

Adapted from a novel by Stephen King, *Firestarter* had all the elements designed to appeal to a girl of eight years. First of all, she was tapped to be the movie's undisputed star, the pyrokinetic title character of Charlie McGee. Secondly, the ensemble cast, which included George C. Scott, Louise Fletcher, and Martin Sheen, was the work of a maestro casting director. (Signing a then twenty-two-year-old Heather Locklear to play Drew's mother was, perhaps, the director's only mistake.) Lastly, Drew's character was not unlike a classic, albeit reluctant, Saturday morning superhero. In the youngster's mind, roles like this didn't come around but once in a lifetime, and she wasn't about to let this big break slip through her still somewhat stubby, little fingers.

The three-and-a-half month filming of *Firestarter* brought with it a great deal of adventure. Drew and her mom were required to move on location to Wilmington, North Carolina. Then, the constant conflagrations that were an integral part of the special effects had Drew living in fear for her life on a daily basis. A similar effect would be produced at night by Stephen King's masterful storytelling.

It was all very heady stuff for an eight-year-old, but surprisingly the most exciting aspect of the production was Drew's friendship with the rather traditional Ward family. Jennifer Ward was a local girl working as Drew's stand-in when the two became pals. When Drew found out that Jenny lived only two doors down from the house that she and her mom had rented for the duration of the shoot, the girls became inseparable.

Drew was swept off her feet by Jenny's ever-so-normal family. A mom, a dad, a brother, a sister . . . even Sunday morning church! Drew couldn't believe her luck. Forget the movie, celebrity be damned, it was the Wards' nuclear family that was Drew's American dream. "It was like having the sister I never had," she said, "so I ended up living with this family . . . and it was like living in a true great family for the first time in my life and it was one of the best experiences."

The child star would blossom into womanhood without ever forgetting the wonderful sleep-overs that she shared with Jenny. In a 1997 story for *US Magazine*, Drew recounted how she and her gal pal "would get into our pajamas and dream of boys to come—at the time it was any member of Duran Duran, with the rude and sole exclusion of Roger—and pretend to play games that seemed appropriate for girls our age. . . . If you want to know my secret desire, it was to have her nightgown. . . . It was just short enough to be politely suggestive. Oh, how I wanted that nightgown. . . . But she wore the garment that I believed was freedom, and I bore the threads that continually tied me down."

When the shoot was completed, Drew was inconsolable. She didn't care two straws for either the glamour of the lights or the action of the cameras—losing the Wards, however, was almost more than her young heart could bear.

Before embarking upon her next cinematic venture, Drew would have to suffer the indignity of going through six whole months at a new school, her third in the three years since she'd made *E.T.* "I went to a regular school but one that would accept me as being in and out [during film shoots] and look the other way," she explained in an interview. "I loved learning, but I was never very good with authority or being patronized, because I pretty much had to raise myself."

Simply put, Drew was considerably more mature than her third-grade counterparts. By working with adults for so long, she'd slowly but surely begun to forget how to relate to her peers. Most of the time, she didn't even see a reason to make the effort. The grown-ups with whom she was on friendly terms were, after all, some of the most attractive and fascinating people in the world, the kind who seemed to be leading some of Hollywood's most charmed existences. A perennial fixture at chichi parties, national talk shows, and local hot spots, Drew rubbed elbows both with the entertainment industry's veterans and the hot, new up-and-comers, such as the shooting stars of the infamous Brat Pack.

"By the time I was eight and a half, I felt like I was some abnormal, crazy girl," she admitted. "I could walk up to the door of any nightclub and they'd say, 'Hi, you're that little girl. Come in.' . . . Around this time I quit hanging out with people my own age. I didn't think I could relate to them or that they could understand the kind of life I had."

Certainly, Drew wasn't completely without friends her own age. But connecting with new kids was growing increasingly difficult with each passing semester. Deep down inside, Drew always knew that the new year would bring a new school, and she'd be back at square one.

The teachers certainly didn't make the work/school transition any easier. "I never really gave of myself in school, because I didn't want to express myself to the teachers, who would just put me down for it," Drew complained. "The only subject I was good at was English. But I would turn in a book report on, say, Henry Miller, and they would give me an F because they didn't consider him a proper writer. But he wrote literature, and they shouldn't have been closed off to certain authors because of what they wrote."

In the end, reconciling her drab classroom existence with her high-profile position in the L. A. club-hopping and premiere-going scene proved too great a feat for Drew. Try as she might, she simply couldn't bring herself to like this thing called school. "I always wanted lice!" she once confessed. "But I never got them—I think because I wanted them for a bad reason, which was to get out of school."

Instead of lice, Drew's "Get Out of Class Free" cards came in the considerably more appealing form of high-paying movie roles. Although it would seem as if Drew was working all the time, she only made about one film per year. As this wasn't nearly enough for her liking, the pint-size starlet jumped at every opportunity to act. Her next would be *Cat's Eye,* the film Stephen King scripted especially with Drew in mind.

Once again, Drew and Jaid were asked to pick up and relocate to Wilmington for the shooting. This time, however, Drew was thrilled to be leaving Los Angeles. The thought of seeing the Wards again had her walking on air for weeks.

Just like the year before, Jennifer Ward was given the job of being Drew's stand-in and the two were quick to get reacquainted. As far as the shoot itself was concerned, *Cat's Eye* did not fall short of Drew's great expectations. After the school year she'd had, Drew badly needed the affirmation of her fellow professionals, and since they were generous in granting it, the little girl was in heaven for the duration of the three-month production schedule.

Of course, the good times could not roll on forever. In fact, in the several years that followed, the filming of *Cat's Eye* would begin to seem a lot like Drew's last hurrah.

THREE

Bad Girl

After the release of *Cat's Eye*, Drew found herself in a dilemma completely foreign to most nine-year-olds. The word around town seemed to be that the young actress was all washed up. None of the three films she'd made after *E.T.* had managed to score at the box office. And in a land where you're only as successful as your last film, *Cat's Eye's* nine million dollar gross did nothing to prevent Drew's star from its decline.

An over-the-hill has-been at nine? Only in Hollywood.

The fact that Drew still had a thriving fan base meant nothing to the movie producers who'd seen their contemporaries stake millions upon her star power and lose. Studio executives suddenly stopped sending scripts to Drew's agent. And when they did think of her, it was usually for small or supporting roles. Tinseltown's change of opinion on the Drew question couldn't have been more unanimous had all the studios held a meeting and decided to blackball the unsuspecting little actress once and for all.

But Drew's professional strife was the least of her

problems. Believe it or not, the cruelty of the Hollywood system was dwarfed by, of all things, the inhu-
manity of her fellow fourth-graders.

As unfathomable as it may seem, the kids at school
were downright horrible to Drew, making her days
nothing short of a living hell. Her cute looks and great
fame didn't stop the schoolyard bullies from singling
her out as fat, ugly "Drew the Poo," laughing at her
every gesture and throwing books and other projectiles
at her as she passed by. Just like most kids in the same
situation, Drew did nothing to thwart her assailants. Instead, she tried to fit in that much more. "You try to
buy the right clothes," she explained, "have the right
style, try to do what some of the other people are doing
to fit in with them. Maybe they'll realize that you are
alike and you do have similarities."

Sadly, all these efforts were for naught. Her classmates were determined to dislike her. Even Drew's attempt at dressing the part ended in disaster when she
came to school wearing a pair of trendy Bermuda shorts
and was labeled a "Cosmic Cow" because they had a
rocket ship design on them. "Grade school for me was
my torture," she recalled. "I mean, I could not win these
people over to save my life. . . . What's worse is when
they're really mean on top of it."

They say that what does not kill us makes us
stronger, and, in time, the bullying that Drew encountered at the hands of her peers would indeed serve to
make her a stronger human being. Before this metamorphosis could take place, however, Drew would try

to drown her sorrows in a pool of alcohol and drugs, and come dangerously close to death in the process.

None but the most avid Drew Barrymore watchers are likely to remember the next stage of Drew's career. From the time she was ten until she turned seventeen, it was her personal life that was the focus of every magazine article and newspaper headline. A party girl at such a young age, Drew first ignored and then struggled with the fact that her fame now rested almost exclusively on the laurels of her childhood.

Although she'd had her infamous "first drink" at eight years old, on the set of *Firestarter,* that had been more of a lark than the catalyst that started her on the path to addiction. Drew's first step into a premature burnout started when she was nine, with a pack of cigarettes and a lie. After splitting a stolen pack in the bathroom with her best friend, Drew learned that she could get away with anything when her mom failed to notice the smell.

Of course, she'd have never tried to smoke had it not been for her robust night life. Seeking to supplement her own lagging social life and keep Drew in the public eye, Jaid had eventually decided that her daughter was responsible enough to attend the industry parties and local hot spots as often as five times a week. Whereas at one time, the two had limited their reveling to the weekends, Drew was now spending an inordinate amount of time on the city's dance floors. Full of smooth-talking and good-looking patrons, most of whom smoked and drank with wanton abandon, the clubs provided the impressionable youngster with a lifestyle that would one day lead her into a rehab clinic.

In her autobiography, Drew recounted how she and her mom would habitually go their separate ways upon arriving at their usual haunt, the très chic Helena's. After getting the VIP treatment from the doormen, Jaid might not see her daughter again until time came to leave. Drew would invariably go off with her best friend—who along with her mother, often accompanied the Barrymores on their nights out—and the two preteens would then proceed to work the room, dancing till all hours, and flirting with the cute older actors who all seemed to know Drew by name.

Although she felt at home at the hippest of Hollywood watering holes, Drew knew that her age set her apart from the movie star crowd just as her work set her apart from the kids at school. In her quest to belong and find acceptance with the beautiful people, she didn't think twice about using the same "when in Rome . . ." technique that had failed to win her admirers at school.

Not long after closet-smoking her first pack of cigarettes, Drew was secretly swilling beers at Rob Lowe's twentieth birthday party. She and her equally precocious sidekick stole one of the open bottles that was standing unattended atop a bar, and smuggled it into a bathroom stall, where they pulled out their cigarettes and set to the task of polishing off the lager. The strange brew left Drew buzzing and she spent the rest of the night on the prowl for more.

This one night of heavy-duty carousing came complete with a make-out session. Although it wasn't Drew's first kiss, it was definitely her least innocent. Like a sorority girl at her first frat party, Drew locked lips with Rob Lowe's twelve-year-old stepbrother in a lover's embrace that reeked of beer and stale cigarettes. In the end, the inebriation proved habit forming. "I started smoking cigarettes when I was nine and a half," she later confessed, "I was, like, smoking constantly and going out and doing everything I could do to be bad. I thought, 'Well, if I smoke cigarettes, I can drink.' At first it was with friends. Just sneaking. I would drink not to have fun—I would drink to get drunk."

Outraged at the tales of Drew's premature escapades, many people have been forced to ask "Where was her mother?" All fingers would inevitably point to Jaid, but to brand her an unfit and irresponsible parent is to over-simplify the Barrymores' complex relationship. "I was there," Jaid insisted, "I was almost disproportionately there because I was there *so* much for her."

Sure enough, wherever Drew went—and she went everywhere—Jaid was right at her side. The days of baby-sitters were a thing of the past, as mother and daughter now seemed to be permanently connected at the hip. Unable to deny Drew's pleas, Jaid had con-vinced herself that she'd have more control over her daughter's actions if they were always together. How could Jaid have known that her ten-year-old was smok-ing cigarettes, drinking, and getting stoned beneath her very nose? In this respect, Jaid was no different than all those so-called responsible parents who take their kids to weddings, dinner parties, and birthday celebrations without ever worrying whether they're picking up bad habits from members of the extended family or sneaking wine off the dinner table.

For all of Drew's transgressions, it wasn't as if the Barrymore household was a free-for-all, anything goes den of iniquity. There were rules, and Jaid expected Drew to follow them. The young girl had to do her homework, restrict herself to a rather conservative curfew, and even perform household chores. In theory, Jaid had it all figured out. "I had tried to be all things to Drew—mother, manager, drill sergeant, friend," Jaid told *People* magazine.

The only problem was that as a friend Jaid could never bring herself to enforce the law that she'd laid down as a drill sergeant. In fact, Drew learned pretty quickly that her mom's admonitions were not to be taken seriously. Jaid's words said one thing, and her actions another. It never failed, if an important event or an exclusive party invitation cropped up, all thoughts of curfews or grounding would disappear as the Barrymore women hurried to dress for the occasion.

In time, besides smoking and drinking, Drew was also ditching school to hang out with her disaffected friends. While much of this truancy and alcohol abuse was Drew's attempt to escape the pain brought on by the malicious group at school, good, old-fashioned teenage rebellion was also partly to blame. As with everything else, Drew progressed into the teen mentality quite early in life. At ten years of age, she was a regular fifteen-year-old—still in dire need of a mother, but loathe to admit it.

Drew's experimentation with marijuana only served to widen the gulf between her mother and herself. For her, smoking pot was just another way to test the boundaries of her independence. "After a while," she recalled, "I started thinking, 'Well, this is getting boring now, so let's try something even better. If I can drink, I can smoke pot. There's nothing to it.'"

Those who wonder where in the world a ten-year-old can score pot are forgetting that Drew was no ordinary ten-year-old. As her introduction to marijuana displayed, the world at large was only too willing to treat her like an adult. "When I was ten and a half," Drew recounted, "I was sitting in a room with a group of young adults who were smoking pot. I wanted to try some, and they said, 'Sure. Isn't it cute, a little girl getting stoned?'"

To make matters worse, the mother of one of Drew's closest friends was also an avid marijuana user. Seeing the weed as a natural alternative to Valium, she smoked pot in front of her daughter and wasn't greedy about sharing her stash with the kids. Whenever Drew slept over at this particular girl's house, which became fairly often after marijuana was factored into the equation, she was sure to get high. Meanwhile, Jaid remained completely oblivious to these nefarious goings-on. In her mind, Drew was just having good, clean pajama-party fun with her little girlfriends. What could be more innocent?

Even the telltale signs of drug abuse that Drew began to exhibit failed to shake Jaid's conception of reality. When Drew told her to stay out of her room, Jaid chalked it up to a privacy issue. When Drew's grades began to slip even further, Jaid attributed it to the boys at school and general boredom. When Drew began to flagrantly disregard her mother's wishes, Jaid just figured that she was willful. Never in her wildest dreams did she think that her baby was all grown-up, and hooked on alcohol and drugs.

Despite all this, Drew was still a child. However, by Hollywood's stringent standards, she was already too old to play the impish roles that had been her trademark only one year ago. Still, she was a known commodity, and scripts for TV movies, sitcoms, and supporting film roles kept on trickling in. Towards the end of fifth grade, Drew was hired to star in a made-for-TV movie called *Babes in Toyland*. While Jaid had had to think long and hard about allowing her movie star of a daughter to make the transition to the small screen, Drew didn't have any qualms about working in television. She just wanted to get back to work, and the sooner, the better.

The film came with the added bonus of being shot in Munich, Germany. During the summer of '86, Drew would have four months to explore the foreign land, along with its people, culture, and countless historical landmarks. Steeped in the camaraderie of a movie shoot, she'd also have ample time to forget all about the mean-spirited gang of peers that had made her life such agony for the past two years.

Sure enough, when she got on the set, Drew immediately felt like she'd been transformed from the ugly duckling to the beautiful swan. Here, people liked and accepted her as one of their own. Within a month, she even had a real-life love interest. While the fifteen-year-old actor wasn't Drew's first boyfriend, he was certainly her most serious.

The whole summer was like one big fantasy, and Drew dreaded waking up to face the demons at school. Luckily, Jaid had thought better of enrolling her daughter at the school that had been the bane of her existence. Cast once again as the new kid in class, Drew didn't know what to expect from her new surroundings, that is until she found that her new school was a junior high and a high school all wrapped up into one. Hanging out with the seniors, cruising in their cars, and smoking dope during lunch periods—now that was more like it.

While most seventeen-year-olds wouldn't get within ten feet of a sixth grader, much less let them into their circle, the older kids made an exception in Drew's case. Interested in her true Hollywood stories and experiences, they drafted her into their clique and recognized her as a fellow partier. For Drew, it was all par for the course. "What made me seem so grown-up was a mixture of fear and confusion," she said. "I was always friends with an older crowd, and I was forced to act a lot older and more sophisticated than I actually was. If you play that game for too long, you forget who you are."

Still trying desperately to fit in, Drew focused all her attention on appearances. Since she didn't look like any of her older friends, she had to come off as being equally brazen, worldly, and, above all, cool. Of course, she wasn't really any of those things on the inside. Her whole public personality was no different from a movie character, a well-orchestrated charade designed to convince the world-at-large and attain some measure of love. But even this facade, which came complete with big Eighties hair and garish makeup, wouldn't have been so bad had drugs and alcohol not played such an integral role. Deep down, Drew was hurting and suffering from an overwhelming sense of loneliness. The fact was that while her school chums may have liked her well enough, she continued to dislike herself.

The entertainment industry was also none too thrilled with Drew at the time. As shallow and superficial as ever, the Hollywood system no longer found Drew's baby fat quite so adorable. In fact, her weight was what caused her to lose most of the parts she went out for. "I was really kind of heavy growing up," she explained. "That was kind of awkward, too. It's amazing how a few extra pounds all of the sudden makes you an entirely different person. It's so wrong, because it's not who you are."

The weight problem was compounded by Drew's ongoing marijuana use. Whether she was hanging out with her high school pals or spending the weekend with her friend (and rumored boyfriend) Eduardo Ponti, son of Sophia Loren and Carlo Ponti, Drew could always be counted upon to take the biggest bong hit. In fact, while all of the world believed that Drew was on the closest of terms with thirteen-year-old Eduardo Ponti, she was actually getting wasted with his older brother, who was a full six years older than she. Naturally, if the kids didn't pass out after a smoke session, they'd invariably maraud the nearest fridge, relieving it of half its contents in the process.

For some time, Drew remained blissfully unaware of central casting's judgmental gaze. Then the bubble burst. Someone had to tell her the truth, and the unsavory job fell to Drew's agent, J. J. Harris. "I looked like a damn butterball, couldn't even get a job because I was so fat," Drew explained. "Nobody would tell me why I couldn't get work, but finally, when I was twelve, my agents sat me down and said, 'You have to lose this weight.' "

Although the news didn't come as any shock—Drew had long since recognized that she wasn't exactly the thinnest girl in school—the fact that her livelihood depended upon her appearance was off-putting, to say the least. From that point on, Drew restricted herself to a low calorie diet, and endured two hours of exercise per day. Although her hard work eventually began to pay off, the self-deprivation often made her irritable and unhappy. "I didn't know anything about good eating," she explained, "so I studied nutrition, and I remember going to McDonald's with my friends and eating watermelon, and they would have Big Macs, and I hated them more than anything in the world."

In this way, Drew managed to shed forty pounds and lose her awkward adolescent image in eight months. She looked every inch the budding starlet that Hollywood expected her to be. But even this success failed to alter the way that she felt about herself. Having lost all that weight, Drew became adamant about staying slim, and more weight-conscious than ever. "It was really difficult after that, because anything I ate, I would immediately gain the weight back. I had to struggle for a long time with that."

To make matters worse, the rest of Drew's life was also spinning completely out of control. Perpetually at loggerheads with her mom and running around with one of the fastest crowds in L.A., Drew was at a breaking point. Had Jaid only known the details of her daughter's daily life, she would have shuddered to think what might come next.

In January of 1988, a few months into her first serious diet, Drew was hired to play a small but important role on *See You in the Morning,* a somewhat somber family drama starring Jeff Bridges and Farrah Fawcett. Drew was to play the adolescent daughter of a young widow who finds love for the second time around. Normally, she would have leapt at the opportunity, but drugs and alcohol had messed with Drew's priorities. Although she'd only done one rather negligible TV movie, *Conspiracy of Love,* since her stint on *Babes in Toyland,* the actress was no longer willing to work at any cost, and, to be perfectly honest, her performance showed it.

Whereas Drew had been flawless in *Irreconcilable Differences* and *Cat's Eye,* to say nothing of *E.T.,* her lackluster turn in *See You in the Morning* was no small indication of the kind of lifestyle she was conducting behind the scenes.

The job required that Drew and her mom relocate to New York City for the four month shoot. Fearing that there would be no one to party with in Manhattan, Drew had been against going from the start. When Jaid forced her hand, thinking that this role would serve her daughter's best interests, Drew was enraged. In her confused state of mind, she went so far as to convince herself that her mom loved the money she made as an actress more than she loved her as a daughter.

The thought of spending four months in close proximity to Jaid scared and depressed Drew. She foresaw nothing but trouble, and she was right.

Desperate to escape her mom, Drew quickly reconnected with some of her East Coast acquaintances and even fell in love. The sleep-overs and the midnight madness started all over again, and she was barely ever at home. The whole trip turned into little more than an aggravated power play between mother and daughter. Jaid would try to set limits on Drew's wild nights of party-going and club-hopping, while Drew would try to assert her independence by defying Jaid at every conceivable turn. After a while, it got so that the two could hardly stand to be in the same room together.

Later in life, Drew would look back and thank Jeff Bridges for helping her see her way clear of the whirlwind into which she'd plunged herself. "That was a very bizarre time in my life," she'd assert. "I was a little confused—a lot confused. And Jeff's kindness kept me grounded."

Of course, profiting by example was not exactly Drew's forte at the time. Back in her hellion days, she wanted nothing other than experience to be her guide. If she was going to learn, it would be from her own mistakes, and no one else's.

Not surprisingly, her mistakes were many. . . . She drank too much; she ignored her mom; she didn't care about her job; she threw herself headlong into an unhealthy romantic relationship . . . but trying cocaine had to be the most dangerous of all. With her highly compulsive personality, Drew was a top candidate for developing a first-rate cocaine addiction. Of course, at thirteen, she was in no position to understand any of this. Nor was she able to recognize the obvious parallels between her behavior and that of her father and grandfather. For Drew, boozing and drugging was all done in the name of fun. Except for boys, nothing else mattered—her mother and her career included.

Drew snorted her first line of cocaine at her school's prom. It happened in May, a month after production on *See You in the Morning* had wrapped. Drew had returned to Los Angeles and fallen right back in with her high school crowd. For all the excitement of being in Manhattan and carrying on her first "mature" relationship, it felt good to be back in familiar surroundings and among her regular crew.

It felt even better after Drew finally yielded to the temptation of cocaine. She was hooked right from the start. For fifteen glorious minutes, the drug relieved Drew of all her cares. She didn't worry about her battle with the bulge or her mother's nagging or her own low self-concept. While she was high, life was beautiful, and so was she. When she'd feel the effects wearing off,

Drew would dip back into her supply and, presto, she was happy again. Cocaine was her cure-all, and from the moment she tried it, Drew could think of nothing else.

When summer vacation arrived, Drew found that she had all the time in the world to indulge her addictions. She'd been relegated to a movie set for so many consecutive summers that she'd almost forgotten what it felt like to do just as she pleased, and not have to worry about an early wake-up call the next morning. Drew was determined to take advantage of this brief respite, even if it killed her.

Her resolve to milk the holiday for all it was worth was strengthened by the fact that she'd been hired to work on yet another movie, and the cameras were set to start rolling in mid-July. That gave Drew one month to do her worst—not a lot of time, but she certainly proved that it could be done.

The moment of reckoning came some two weeks into Drew's vacation, on June 28, 1988. She went to a drive-in movie with some friends, and proceeded to embark upon a beer-drinking binge. The group stayed out into the wee hours, way past Drew's curfew. But breaking the house rule turned out to be the least of her infractions—in a drunken stupor, she actually called her mom and ordered her to find other accommodations for the night.

"When I got home," Drew told *People* magazine, "I confronted my mother and screamed, 'What the hell are you doing here?' I wanted her out of the house—I said it was my turn to be Mom. She just stood there blankly, looking at me like I was the biggest asshole in the world. She wasn't feeding into my shit, and that only made things worse. So I started throwing things . . . I [went] to get another beer and was huffing and puffing and swearing at my mother when the front door swung open. 'Oh, shit, the cops,' I thought. But coming through the door was a friend I had cut off contact with because she had checked into a rehabilitation program to get sober, and that wasn't cool. By that time, I could hardly walk or function. She and her mother pulled me into their car."

"Where are you taking me?" Drew demanded.

"The hospital."

"Good answer," thought the juvenile delinquent as she silently thanked her lucky stars. It could have been worse, they might have said "jail." Of course, the night's final destination would not be just any old hospital. At long last, and just in the nick of time, Drew was on the road to rehab.

FOUR

Junkie

For as long as she could remember, Drew had thought of herself as being somehow different from everybody else. She didn't have a father. She didn't fit in with kids her own age. She wasn't expected to abide by any real rules. She had to work for a living. She had the worst problems. She was beyond help. The list went on and on.

At ASAP Family Treatment Center, Drew learned how wrong she'd been. Not only wasn't her situation different, but it was almost exactly identical to those of the other addicts at the clinic. In rehab parlance, Drew was an "addict/alcoholic," and if she thought that she had it bad, she had only to listen to the horror stories of her fellow patients to grasp the meaning of the word "pain."

Not that Drew's physical and mental state weren't in dire need of assistance. In fact, Drew's ASAP counselor, Betty Wyman, recalled that "she was so sick, sick, sick when I met her. I thought, 'What a sad kid.'"

Sad, definitely, but beyond help, certainly not.

When Jaid discovered how far gone Drew actually

was, she couldn't believe that she'd allowed her daughter's life to spiral so completely out of control. Her worst suspicions had finally been confirmed, and upon hearing of the extent of Drew's drinking and the frequency of her drug-using, the inconsolable mom cried tears of pure disbelief. "Like most parents, I had no idea what was going on," she ruefully admitted. "So where was I? The question is a shocker since our lives have been intertwined like braids, almost like the two of us against the world."

But the concerned mother couldn't deny her daughter's own admissions of guilt. Yes, she'd drunk something like fifteen beers that evening alone. Yes, she'd smoked pot. Yes, she'd done coke. Drew was so drunk the night her mom and friends brought her into the hospital that she couldn't even make her way to her designated room.

After waking up from what she'd been inclined to think was a bad dream, Drew found that she was indeed confined to a drug rehabilitation program. She couldn't hang out with her friends; she couldn't enter into romantic liaisons with boys; she couldn't stay up past ten o'clock; she couldn't smoke in her room; she couldn't drink; she couldn't do drugs . . . basically, life as she knew it was history.

Instead, the recovering addict/alcoholic was required to attend group therapy. There she'd have to listen to other addicts and alcoholics recount their problems, and even share some of her own. At first, and for a long time thereafter, Drew resisted the helping hand held out by the ASAP staff. She knew perfectly well that she'd be out in less than two weeks due to her upcoming film shoot. Sure, it was a frightening wake-up call, but in the back of her mind, Drew couldn't help thinking that twelve days wasn't such a big deal—she'd tell them what they wanted to hear, and would be out in no time.

The days that Drew put in at the ASAP treatment facility turned out to be time well spent. Although her stay hadn't been long, she was already beginning to feel safe within the confines of the center's strict rules and daily routine. It had taken some doing, but Drew was actually starting to open up and let down her guard in therapy and group sessions.

For the sake of her career, however, the treatment had to be interrupted. Some months earlier, Drew had won her first "grown-up" role in *Far From Home*. She was to play a teenage girl who, along with her father, is stranded without gasoline in a small, trailer-park town that is being stalked by a mysterious killer. The movie would focus a great deal of attention on her character's budding sexuality, featuring Drew in quite a few bikini shots. Providing the child star with the ultimate opportunity to transition into more mature roles, the movie was one commitment that Drew and her mother intended to keep.

To this end, Drew was pulled out of ASAP and deposited on location in the small town of Gerlach, Nevada. Fortunately, she wasn't alone. Besides Jaid, Drew also had the companionship of a former ASAP patient. If she ever felt the desire to drink or act out, she could go to this woman to discuss her feelings and ride out the craving.

Temptation, as it turned out, was right around the corner. In Gerlach, Drew had rediscovered the joys of filmmaking, but when the production moved to the gambling town of Carson City, Nevada, Drew was back to her old tricks. Unable to resist the lure of the bright lights, she'd tease her hair, glop on the makeup, and don her slinkiest dresses for wild nights on the casino floor. When she said that she was twenty-two, she wasn't hard to believe, and those who've seen the thirteen-year-old's work in *Far from Home* know why. Drew was a beautiful and very full-figured girl, one of those eighth graders who develop early and cause a stir every time they walk down the hallway. Although she may have hated her 34 DD bra size, it came in handy when trying to pull the wool over the vigilant eyes of a pit boss.

"I dressed up and turned on my Scarlett O'Hara, sexy-girl act at the casinos, where they really believed I was twenty-two," Drew admitted. "A crew member let me throw the dice on the craps table. Then I went to the blackjack table and turned twenty dollars into two hundred, only to lose it all again. I started getting back into that party girl habit, hanging out with people who were drinking. I managed to stay sober. But it was a real struggle."

Drew's newfound sobriety manifested itself in her performance. Although it had only been a few months since she'd finished filming *See You in the Morning*, it was almost as if she was a different, and much improved, actress. Although neither movie would fare well at the box office, *Far from Home* would at least give Drew something to be proud of.

Despite this small step forward, Drew still had a long way to go, both as an actor and as a human being, when she returned to Los Angeles that September. Since she'd been clean and sober for two and a half months, Drew didn't understand why she had to go back to ASAP. But go back she did.

This time, however, her stay would be even shorter than her last. After six days at the hospital, she had to leave for New York. There was no getting around it. Not only did Drew want to audition for a play, but *See You in the Morning* was in postproduction, and she was contractually obligated to loop some lines of dialogue.

Oddly enough, as much as she claimed to dislike ASAP, Drew was apprehensive about leaving. She had friends in Manhattan, and this time, her ASAP sponsor wouldn't be there to protect her.

In retrospect, Drew's fears were right on target. Upon her arrival in New York, she wasted no time before touching base with her old enablers, an eighteen-year-old model/actress and an uptown boy with whom she'd grown intimate some eight months earlier. For all her efforts to steer clear of alcohol, Drew's inner wild child was dying to break free. It was this repressed urge to self-destruct that pushed Drew into all kinds of dangerous situations. Outwardly, she made a big show of not drinking and not getting high, but as she continued to seek out the fast times and night life, it seems as though Drew was just looking for a good excuse to slip up.

On September 15, she got her wish.

That night, Drew and her girlfriend set out to paint the town. Drew hadn't touched a drop of alcohol or smoked anything other than cigarettes for nearly three months, and the girls were just going to dance the night away at some trendy New York nightclub. At first, everything went according to plan. Drew even congratulated herself on her strong willpower when she responded in the negative to a standard ladies room question—"Do you do blow?"

The test of will, however, was far from over. Instead of letting it go at that, the girls proceeded to snort their cocaine right under Drew's very nose. Watching them inhale line after tantalizing line, she felt a strong urge to join in the merrymaking. Finally, Drew could take it no longer. But instead of fleeing the premises as her therapists had advised her to do, Drew pulled back her golden hair, bent over the counter, and proceeded to snort two lines of the noxious white powder.

It should have felt good. She should have been walking on air. Instead, she felt like a wretched failure. Three months of clean living had just gone up her nose. It was all over. Now, there was only one thing left to do—more cocaine. "I figured as long as I'd stepped over the line, I might as well go all out," Drew recalled.

The whole experience was nothing less than a classic relapse. Within minutes, Drew had homed in on a dealer and scored a gram of cocaine. For the next seven hours, she and her friend were flying high. The girls didn't come down until they arrived back at Drew's house at 7:30 A.M. and saw a worried Jaid waiting up for them. Lying through her teeth, Drew told her mom that she'd spent the night at her friend's. Jaid believed her, and it could have ended right there had Drew's need for attention not reared its desperate head.

The events that followed can only be viewed as a cry for help. With her partner in crime at her side, Drew stole a credit card from her mom's purse and took a cab to LaGuardia Airport. The two conspirators then used the card to buy airline tickets to Los Angeles. It was crazy, but then again, at the time, so was Drew.

When they got back to Los Angeles, Drew called her mom to let her know that she'd be home soon.

"That's it, I'm calling the cops," said Jaid.

Drew was livid. She hadn't figured on her mom catching on so soon.

"Do whatever the hell you want," she seethed. "See if I care."

As if to prove that her mom's words had made no impression, Drew and her friend got into Jaid's BMW and went on a shopping spree, buying more coke as well as hundreds of dollars worth of clothes. Tired from all the shopping, the girls returned home and snorted most of their newly bought cocaine. They were feeling no pain when two detectives walked through the doors and apprehended them both. Walking out of her house in handcuffs, Drew could only think that her worst nightmare was finally coming true.

Of course, Jaid would never have called the police on

her own daughter. These were private investigators, hired with the express purpose of taking Drew back to the hospital before she could do any more damage to herself. No one, but no one, was to know of this affair.

Upon learning that she was not headed for jail, Drew was again awash in relief. This feeling quickly turned to anger when the private eyes began probing her about the making of *E.T.* But if this line of questioning upset Drew, she hadn't seen anything yet. "When we arrived at the admitting hall . . . believe it or not, they asked me for my autograph."

The party was now over. Drew's days of skipping out on her rehab program for work purposes were at an end. A menace both to herself and to society, she would leave the hospital only at such a time as the staff deemed her good and ready, and not a moment sooner. Such was Drew's predicament, and like it or not, she was going to have to deal with it.

Was she going to wing her way through the program, as so many rehab-bound stars have done before and since, or was she going to buckle down and do some serious self-improvement?

In the initial week of treatment, it became evident that Drew was no longer content to sweep her problems under the proverbial rug. Her first step was to admit that she was, in fact, an addict/alcoholic. At length, she'd realized the obvious—the tag was not a joke designed for her amusement, but the cold, hard truth.

From this moment on, Drew was able to accept the staff's help and tackle her issues head-on. Her father's absence, her mother's ambiguous role in her life, her maternal grandfather's recent passing, her own deep-seated feelings of worthlessness . . . all were addressed and dealt with accordingly.

But lest anyone think that sorting through this morass of emotions was easy, they need only consider the length of time that it took Drew to complete the program. She'd been admitted on September 17 and was not discharged until December 21. That's more than three months of round-the-clock therapy and emotional upheaval. In that time, Drew had cried buckets of tears, she'd screamed her vocal chords raw in mother-daughter therapy sessions, she'd even lost an additional twenty-five pounds from the sheer stress of the experience.

Day by day, the hospital taught Drew how to cope with regular life. Instead of denying the facts and running for the shelter of inebriation, she learned how to identify her feelings and act upon them. It had taken everything she had to turn her internal life around in the span of three months, but in the end, Drew came out of the hospital a survivor.

Her years of hiding behind a wall were now a relic of the past, both in the figurative and the literal sense. For no sooner had Drew been released than the whole world was apprised of her struggle. "Toward the end of one of my hospital stays, a person from the *National Enquirer* broke into the hospital and saw me there," she explained. "And it was he who created the story."

E.T. STAR IN COCAINE AND BOOZE CLINIC—AT 13! THE SHOCKING UNTOLD STORY!

Thanks to the *Enquirer,* Drew made front-page news on January 3, 1989. The story's publication sent seismic shock waves throughout the United States. Drew's former *E.T.* costar, Henry Thomas, echoed the prevailing sentiments when he stated, "It's kind of shocking that this little girl you knew when she was six and in pigtails was doing cocaine. I felt very bad and was very concerned."

The media's conjecture and speculation ran rampant. The paparazzi came out in full force. By week's end, everyone knew the young star's sad story. For Drew, who was still vulnerable after her hospital stay, standing in the eye of the controversy was almost more trauma than she could handle. A few years later, she'd relate to young Macaulay Culkin's well-publicized situation, saying that "people have to realize that when that poor kid is at home and people are saying those terrible things about him and his family, it hurts him a lot."

So, was the worst over, or had Drew's troubles only just begun? At this point, it was still far too early to tell.

"These are your options: You can completely deny it, or you can admit it and go on with your life and never talk about it again. Or you are in a position of power to speak your mind and help other people."

Sitting across the desk from her agent, a pensive Drew listened intently to every word. But she didn't have to think twice about her reply.

"I think you all know what choice I'm going to take," she said.

At ASAP, Drew had learned that coming clean both

with herself and with others is an integral part of staying clean. There was no way that she was going to revert to her childhood patterns and lie to the whole world. Whatever the consequences of her actions, Drew would tell the truth. "What was important to me was my recovery. I think that people are constantly covering up for what they've done, and I didn't want to be like that. I didn't want to be a coward and say, 'I made some mistakes, but everything is fine.'"

To this end, Drew agreed to speak with *People* magazine. Holding nothing back, she recounted the recent events that had led her into ASAP in graphic detail. She talked about her drug use, she revealed the dysfunctions of her family, she didn't even hide the fact that she stole her mom's credit card and used it to fly cross-country on a juvenile crime spree. Not surprisingly, the support for Drew's candor was by no means unanimous. Indeed, many were the voices that cried "spoiled brat."

For her part, Drew would not be intimidated. The only people who mattered to her were those who were struggling with the same addictions and looking to her as a role model of recovery.

Having told her side of the story, Drew was ready to dramatize it on national television. A CBS Schoolbreak Special titled *The Ring 15 and Getting Straight* just happened to be in production around the time Drew left ASAP. Starring fellow troubled child stars Tatum O'Neal and Corey Feldman, the movie was shot at the ASAP center and revolved around the process of recovering from addiction. Mirroring much of Drew's own experience, the part of an addict/alcoholic/bulimic in

Getting Straight helped her open up about her problems and primed her for the ultimate challenge that still lay ahead.

Little Girl Lost, the memoir that Drew would coauthor with Todd Gold (the same *People* magazine reporter to whom she'd first recounted her story), came about as a direct result of Drew's willingness to speak out. As it turned out, Drew's efforts on behalf of drug- and alcohol-addicted teens everywhere had not gone unnoticed. America's biggest publishing houses had been hanging on the young actress's every word. Every editor worthy of his nameplate was hooked on Drew's story and determined to get her name on a book deal. "Then all these different publishing companies call—it was *buzzing,*" recalled Drew. "They were going, 'She's got recovery, she's got time, she's got a great story— please, let us write her book.'"

Since Drew already had her hands full juggling Alcoholics Anonymous meetings, school work, and the turmoil of adolescence, the thought of writing a book was not a little bit daunting. Still, she wanted to make a difference, and if that meant sacrificing her time and privacy, so be it. Her decision made, Drew had no problem picking a publisher for her work. "The reason I chose Simon & Schuster as my publisher was that they were more interested in what I had to say than what they *wanted* me to say," she explained.

If she was going to tell her full story, she was going to tell it her way. The book would not be a tawdry tell-all. Many names would be changed to protect the not-so-innocent. The central truths of Drew's problematic existence, however, would be revealed in all their complexity. Drew could only hope that people would not judge her too harshly for the mistakes she made on the way to growing up too fast.

In the spring of '89, it looked as if Drew had finally gotten her life under control. Almost three months had passed since she'd walked out of the ASAP hospital dormitory. She was immersed in writing an optimistic book about "her descent into addiction—and out again." She was studying hard and bringing home high grades. She got well-paying jobs as a doorkeeper at a few nightclubs. She even felt strong enough to start dating again, and was often seen arm in arm with hot, young star Corey Feldman. This last bit of trivia, however, might have been cause for great concern had we known then what we know now—namely, that Feldman was not averse to either cocaine or heroin. In fact, only one year hence, the promising actor's once thriving career would be curtailed by a scandalous drug bust.

Although the relationship between Drew and Corey would not last two months, it would serve as a lasting symbol of the dangers that go with coming too close to the fire. The fact was that while Drew did her best to stay away from drugs, she still felt compelled to hang out with both social and regular users. As she would soon learn, this could only mean one thing: she was dry, but not sober. "When you're dry, you don't have the chemicals," elaborated Drew, "but you're doing the same old patterns as when you were loaded. When somebody puts a joint in front of your face, it's easy to say, 'Okay.'"

To her credit, Drew never again succumbed to the sinister allure of cocaine. Nor did she ever consider throwing in the towel on her recovery. Even on the three separate occasions that she smoked marijuana, Drew was still struggling to stay clean and promising herself that it would never happen again. The guilt, however, would not let her be. Ever since she smoked her first post-ASAP joint, entering her AA meetings and laying claim to a sobriety that was still outside her reach made her feel like a fraud and a liar. The self-loathing engendered by this deception only set her up for more failure. Whether she knew it or not, that first joint had put Drew right back on the road to ASAP.

Everything came to a head on Independence Day '89. By this time, Drew had gotten her mother's consent to move out of their house. But sharing a West Hollywood apartment with her friend did not turn out to be the liberating experience she'd thought it would be. Apparently, this was not a roommate match made in heaven. Neither did the distance improve Drew's relationship with her mom. If that wasn't bad enough, she'd gained ten pounds since her release from the hospital and, worse still, had done marijuana without telling anyone. All told, Drew felt like a miserable failure.

To further complicate matters, she had received a devastating phone call from her father. The last time the two had spoken, Drew was trying to resolve her abandonment issues at ASAP; the last time they'd met, she was six years old. But none of this impeded John Barrymore from calling his fourteen-year-old daughter at her new apartment and asking for a loan. "If I had been in a rational state," confessed Drew, "I probably wouldn't have been suckered into him, but I was so frazzled, I just went, 'No!' and flew off the handle. Everything was coming down on me."

In her desperation, Drew wound up getting stoned for the third time since rehab. But that only made her feel worse. Later that night, she called her mom for some moral support, but none was forthcoming. Instead, Jaid informed her daughter that she was going to New York to move some belongings out of their old apartment. Drew felt the walls closing in on her; it was just as if she was six years old again, with neither a father nor a mother to guide her.

The next day found Drew depressed, but intent on putting aside her problems and enjoying a good Fourth of July barbecue with her friends. But just as she was making her plans, she found out that her roommate, with whom she'd wanted to spend the holiday, was mad at her. This was the straw that broke the proverbial camel's back. Drew felt like she had no one, that everyone to whom she'd reached out had rejected her and that she could never be happy again. "I thought, 'My dad hates me; I'm fat and ugly; I've got no money; I'm living on my own; nobody likes me; I can't stand this!' "

Overcome by grief and self-pity, she called everyone she could think of to no avail. Her mom was not home, her ASAP therapists were nowhere to be found, and her own tears just wouldn't stop gushing. Someone had to care, someone had to pay attention—and if they didn't, she knew just how to make them. Drew recounted, "If a gun was there, you know, I might have shot myself, I don't know. I grabbed a knife . . . went in the living room, and I cut [my wrist], and right then my friend walked in, freaked out, and rushed me to the hospital."

Less than a month later, the *National Enquirer* would again alert the whole of the English-speaking world to Drew's desperate lot. The headline read, E.T. STAR, 14, ATTEMPTS SUICIDE BY SLASHING WRIST.

Suicide attempt, nervous breakdown, morbid depression, relapse, cry for help, whatever you call it, this latest catastrophe was, paradoxically enough, the best thing that could have happened to Drew. No matter how much she'd tried to play off her three breaches of sobriety as isolated incidents, she had not managed to fool herself. Psychologically, she was still hooked on drugs, and she knew it.

Returning to the quiet comfort of the ASAP treatment center was just what Drew needed. She'd done a great job of putting up a brave front and keeping up with her therapy, but her life these past six months had been in a state of utter disarray. The three months that she'd spent at the hospital had gone a long way toward helping Drew break her addictions, but she was still a few therapy sessions shy of solving the problems that had caused her to abuse drugs in the first place.

While Drew's commitment to working through her various issues was strong, she couldn't do it alone. This time, Jaid would have to do her part. For years and years, the rapport between mother and daughter could only be characterized as codependent. There were no boundaries, no mutual respect, and no emotional support. Nonetheless, it was the single most important relationship in Drew's life. Something had to be done to mend the strained family tie, and the hospital staff suggested that Jaid get some counseling as well.

Finally, Drew was able to see how much her mother cared about her and about their relationship. This realization, so hard to come by, was crucial to her recovery. Three months after her readmission to ASAP, Drew was once again set free. Correction, make that *almost* free.

Just to be on the safe side, the hospital therapists had recommended that Drew stay at the home of David Crosby and his wife Jan Dance. At one time, Crosby had been as renowned for his drug addictions as he'd been for his rock group Crosby, Stills, and Nash. But in October 1989, when Drew came out of rehab for the second and final time, the Crosbys had long since become the very epitome of model citizenship. In fact, Jan had been acting as Drew's AA sponsor ever since Drew's first foray out of the hospital.

For the next three months, Drew would have twenty-four hour access to her sponsor. What's more, she'd at long last find out what it's like to have both a male and a female authority figure in her life. The Crosby home was like a halfway house, ideally suited to helping Drew readjust to life on the outside. As she'd already learned, the traumatic transition from the rigid regimen of ASAP to the lax ways of the Hollywood scene had the power to undermine much of the good done by the program. This being Drew's second shot at well-being, no one wanted to take any chances.

By the time her three months with Jan and David

were up, Drew had effected a complete about-face. "It was good for Drew to be in a more conventional kind of house," attested her counselor, Betty Wyman. "My sense is that she thrived and blossomed at Jan and David's in a way I hadn't seen before."

Jaid was also surprised by the transformation. Her daughter was back to her old self, she seemed happy, she no longer hung out at bars and nightclubs, she was excited about acting again and, best of all, she was completely drug and alcohol free. "The first time she came out [of rehab]," recalled Jaid in *People*, "we both looked at each other, going, 'Oh, God, I hope this works.' But she wants it now. I think she's gonna be all right."

Thanks largely to her time with David and Jan, Drew's attitude toward boys had also become a whole lot healthier. Whereas at one time, she wasn't content without a love interest, Drew was finally able to look at her need for love and see it for what it really was: an attempt to replace her father. "Basically, what I was looking for in men or boys was acceptance," she explained. "You want to feel pretty, you want to feel loved, you want to be hugged, you want to feel adored. You want to feel that grounding of security that sometimes only men can give you, you know? And sometimes that gets out of control. It certainly did with me."

Far older and wiser than her fourteen years, Drew was ready to face the world. But was the world ready for the new and improved Drew?

FIVE

Has Been

Not so long before, Drew thought she had it all figured out. She even thought that she knew how her autobiography was going to end—with the words "at least I'm alive." Since that time, her biography had had to be amended to include her second trip to the hospital, she'd done another big interview with *People* magazine to update her continuing saga as well as to respond to the half-truths printed in the tabloids, and she'd finally kicked her drug habit once and for all. Now, Drew knew only that she didn't know, and that was okay.

When her book, *Little Girl Lost,* appeared in bookstores in 1990, the young author was almost afraid to show her face. "When it came out, I was very nervous," she admitted. "For the first two days I stayed in my house." She'd poured so much of her heart into those pages that the slightest criticism or sign of rejection would have cut her to the quick. "It was so scary to put myself out there and be so vulnerable to people, especially the people who just want a nasty story and don't care about you at all. But the truth is, with me you always know what you're getting. I imagine it takes a lot more energy to hide and not be yourself."

Drew needn't have worried. Before long, the results were in: her sad story was flying off the shelves faster than bookstores could stock it. A few weeks after her book debuted, she got a phone call from her publisher. "I just want to congratulate you on being a best-selling author."

To be sure, the high sales figures were considered a great coup in the book publishing sector; in Drew's world, however, the only thing that mattered was the response of her target audience. "The point was that I reached *tons* of people," she enthused. "People would come up to me and say, 'I just read your book. I've been honest to my parents. I finally told them how I felt about them.' "

Having set out to help as many people as possible, Drew couldn't have asked for a better outcome. She'd accomplished her greatest dream: to make a difference. And so what if some people only read her book for the gossip? Who cared if her confessions caused a few Hollywood honchos to cross her off their lists? By coming out and telling her story, she'd accomplished what often takes whole lifetimes to achieve.

The thought of all the good she'd done would have to sustain Drew through the choppy waters that still lay ahead. Truth is, despite the optimistic sound bites she gave to the intrusive press corps, Drew was still fighting for dear life. As she later revealed, the publication of her book coincided with yet another personal low point. "I was miserable . . ." she related.

"My life was like an open book, you know. No pun intended."

Indeed, Drew had many reasons to feel blue. First and foremost of these was her total and complete inability to get an acting job. For a while, she had let the matter drop, content to wait for the dust to settle. Busy working her recovery program, she had hardly noticed that producers were no longer beating a path to her door. Alas, Drew's interest in acting returned much sooner than Hollywood's interest in her. After all, the movies had been Drew's stock-in-trade for so long. Not only did she not know any other way of life, but she'd worked very hard to build a career. To realize that she was considered a has-been by many was a rude awakening. In the callous circles of film casting, conventional wisdom had Drew cast in the role of an unhirable disgrace, maybe even a joke.

Opening herself up to such censure time after time could have driven Drew right back into the addicts' ward. "I thought I'd never work again," she said. But instead of reaching for the nearest drug dealer, Drew displayed her remarkable strength by going about the business of living just as if she was a regular out-of-work actress, and not a onetime box-office champ. "I had to prove myself," she said. "I knew it would be tough, and I knew there would be disbelievers and I knew I had to keep going. Even when it didn't feel good."

There were no two ways about it, Drew *had* to keep trying. After a brief posttherapy attempt to cohabit with her mother, she came to the conclusion that she and her mother "were too codependent to live together any-more." For all her counselors' efforts to convince her that she was still a child, Drew could not shake the conviction that she was old enough to make her own decisions. Having gone through hell and lived to tell about it, she believed that she'd earned her adult's stripes fair and square.

As an adult, albeit one still enrolled in high school, Drew found that work was no longer a matter of choice. After moving out of the condo she'd shared with Jaid, Drew got her own tiny apartment, where she could come and go as she pleased, entertain whomever and whenever she liked, and generally lead her life her way. Best of all, this new living arrangement came complete with mom's seal of approval. "That's been a huge big deal," Drew commented on the relocation, "but I think my mom and I have worked out the move. It's not like I don't see her or talk to her every day."

Problem was, apartment living did not come cheap. Going to school and getting rejected at auditions would not pay Drew's way. Swallowing her pride, she made like any other aspiring actress, rolled up her sleeves and got to waiting tables. "I didn't know how I was going to pay my rent," Drew lamented. "I worked at a coffeehouse and kept going on auditions and living in a small apartment and praying every day."

Visitors and residents of Los Angeles alike were treated to a most odd celebrity-sighting upon entering the trendy coffee shop where this world famous teen donned a happy face and poured java to paying customers on a daily basis. Trying to work as smug curiosity-seekers whispered and snickered in her wake couldn't have been pleasant, but those were the breaks and Drew wasn't above rolling with the punches. "You have to do everything," she said of her coffeehouse job, "clean the bathroom, wash the dishes, meet the muffin man at 6 A.M."

If her professional life was something of a wash, her school life was an absolute disaster. In fact, according to Drew, "It was awful. People wouldn't even talk to me . . . it was a lonely experience."

Lonely and, like most things in Drew's life, very painful. Since no one ever bothered to get to know her, Drew often wound up sitting alone in the cafeteria, desperately hoping that someone would come up to talk to her. Eventually, someone did. Her name was Jenny, and she, too, was an outcast. "I made friends with the girl who was like me—whom no one wanted to hang out with. We ended up being great friends," Drew recalled. "I used to feel her pain and how she felt being awkward. And I knew one day she'd be so much more interesting than these girls who were more popular and beautiful and hated us."

Although Drew dismisses the theory that her classmates were either jealous of or intimidated by her fame, what else can one make of the ill will that she encountered at the hands of the popular girls' clique. At one point, Drew actually had reason to hope that her luck was about to change. It was the day that a cheerleader approached her and invited her to practice with the squad after school. For the rest of the afternoon, Drew was on cloud nine. Smiling to herself, she entertained thoughts of her impending acceptance and popularity. Could things really turn around that easily?

Hardly. "That day at practice, the most popular girl in my school saw fat little me arrive in the gym," Drew recalled. "She stopped midcheer to scream, 'What is SHE doing here?' I was mortified, and then this girl insisted, 'Get that idiot out of here!' I ran out in tears. It is still the most humiliating moment of my entire life. I will never forget it."

Reviled both at work and at school, Drew had every reason in the world to run for the shelter of drugs and drink, and only one reason not to—someday, she was going to make it and she wanted to be perfectly lucid when that day came.

For all the negativity surrounding her, Drew was learning to love herself with the help of her friends. As usual, the people with whom she was closest were in their late teens and twenties and well beyond the high school scene. Drew's longtime friend, eighteen-year-old actress Ele Keats, would do her best to divert our young heroine from her not-so-happy lot by taking her to shopping malls and low-key night spots.

On February 22, 1990, her fifteenth birthday, Drew was feted at the Donovan-Leitch-owned, and thus supertrendy, Grotto room. Blowing out her candles and laughing along with guests such as Keanu Reeves and Scott Baio, Drew looked as carefree as a kid on the last day of school. And perhaps she finally was. For despite the many problems still left to work out, Drew finally trusted herself to make the right decisions.

Drew's fifteenth year would see her implementing sweeping changes in her life. But everything she did, she did with only one goal in mind: her own happiness and well-being. That in itself was quite a change from the self-destructive Barrymore of yesteryear.

The first sign of Drew's total life overhaul was the petition she entered in juvenile court asking to be emancipated from her parents. If the judge ruled in Drew's favor, she would become an adult, with all the rights and privileges thereof, in the eyes of the legal system. Her parents would no longer be able to make decisions for her, and she'd be able to work without being governed by child-labor laws. After waiting months and months for her case to come to court, Drew was rewarded for her patience. "The judge said he couldn't turn back the clock, he could only turn it forward," Drew recounted to *Teen*. "I remember thinking, 'Thank God! I don't want to go back there!' I just knew: I am all of my responsibility. And I liked that feeling."

At long last, Drew was in control of her own destiny. So, what was her first act as an adult? To drop out of high school, what else? "I dropped out rather early, which I don't recommend," she's since cautioned.

That was Drew, the role model, talking. Perhaps in her situation, dropping out made perfect sense. Not only did she not have any friends to brighten up her seemingly interminable school days, but she also couldn't summon the will to concentrate on the lectures. Most important, Drew was well aware of the fact that she wasn't going to be a doctor, a lawyer, or an accountant. For her, it was Hollywood or bust. If only someone would take a chance and hire her! But the machinations of the film industry were beyond Drew's control.

What wasn't out of reach was a new self-image. Ever since she was twelve, when she'd been told that her weight was to blame for her career slump, Drew had been struggling to keep fashionably trim. It wasn't until she was fifteen that she learned to accept her body, and gave up dieting forever.

"One day I was sitting in my living room. I was fifteen, I was in my new apartment, and I really wanted to eat my favorite food, macaroni and cheese," she later recounted. "And I was worried because I had this audition the next day, and I had to stay thin. And I just said, 'I'm gonna eat and I don't care what happens. I'm just tired of living my life feeling guilty about every single bite of food I put in my mouth.' And ever since then . . . I've pretty much eaten whatever I wanted and remained the same weight. . . . Some people say that being fat might be psychological. And I believe in my heart that it was with me. The minute I stopped feeling guilty, I was able to eat what I wanted when I wanted, some bad foods and some good, and I was okay."

With her weight a nonissue, Drew was able to concentrate on more important things, such as matters of the heart. Always looking for love, Drew was like so many young girls who can never quite be content without a guy in their lives. Her time at ASAP had opened her eyes to the root of this pattern, but it could not undo the early abandonment that had sparked Drew's need for security. Being in love was Drew's be-all and end-all, and now that she was involved in a serious relationship with twenty-four-year-old Leland Hayward (the two were even reported to be engaged), she was finally able to say, "I am in love, really in love." The phrase would become a favorite of Drew's. As most of her fans probably know, the relationship with Hayward would fizzle out soon enough. In fact, Drew would go on to fall in love with another, and then another after that, and so on. The stories of her many loves would make for great copy time and again. But, for the moment, Drew's love life was in high gear and she couldn't have been happier.

Movie roles did not come easier with the arrival of Drew's sweet sixteen. Apparently, becoming an emancipated minor had done nothing to bring the big-time producers around. If anything, Drew was seen as even more of a problem child than ever before. "This business is very unfair to young people," she would later observe, "especially when they're trying to make the transition. It's not fair to make people feel guilty for growing up."

So, in 1991, the only headline printed about Drew Barrymore was that she had a major crush on *Beverly Hills 90210* hunk, Jason Priestley. While DREW BARRYMORE WANTS HER 90210 MAN may have sounded a bit racy, it certainly paled in comparison to the kind of news Drew used to make. Actually, the fan letter that Drew sent to Priestley was hardly the most noteworthy aspect of her year—that honor would have to go to her breast reduction surgery.

Ever since she'd blossomed into premature womanhood at the age of twelve, Drew had been acutely conscious of her enormous bra size. Back when Drew was still a working actress, her 34 DD measurement had been the cause of great consternation for wardrobe departments charged with the task of squeezing her womanly body into a girly costume. "You should have seen the size of them," she exclaimed to one interviewer. "One more Dolly Parton comment and I was about to lose my mind! I completely lost my identity. People would never look me in my eyes. They'd go, 'Boy, you're really growing up,' looking straight at my breasts."

Although Drew would one day make light of her predicament, at the time it was no laughing matter. Indeed, she was so uncomfortable with her bust size that she chose surgery, with all its accompanying risks, rather than go through one more day of hunching her shoulders and wearing baggy clothes. In the final analysis, Drew claimed that the procedure "was the most wonderful choice I've ever made. All of a sudden this thing that was terribly depressing and scary and embarrassing was not a problem any more."

Free of the physical and psychological burden, Drew felt like a new woman despite the persistent sputtering of her career. Her determination to reclaim her rightful place among the Hollywood elite, however, had never been stronger. By using the lull in her acting activity to work on rebuilding her life, she became virtually unstoppable. Suddenly, Drew wasn't out there trying to impress people anymore. She came to auditions as a woman secure in her talents, not as a girl in search of validation. And her new passion and attitude would soon bear fruit.

SIX

Grunge Goddess

In the early 1990s, the face of American pop culture was undergoing a radical reconstruction. The big hair and big spending of the Me Generation were now strictly for the history books. Wall Street was no longer buzzing; heavy metal was no longer cool; and even Donald and Ivana Trump, the power couple of the '80s, had broken up. The time to accept the stock market crash of 1987 and the ensuing economic recession had finally arrived.

This acceptance quickly led to a new aesthetic, one that was more in keeping with the decidedly dour spirit of the times. The starved waif models, the thrift-shop chic clothing, and the depressed rantings of the Seattle sound embodied the not-so-pleasant reality of sweeping unemployment and morbidly low hopes for the future. For the first time in decades, U.S. high school students came of age thinking that they would not have it as good as their Baby Boomer parents. This population of disaffected teens were branded Generation X, a name that was supposed to characterize the apathy and general discontent that defined the demographic. Now, had the movie studios purposely tried to cast the role of Generation X Icon, they couldn't have done any better than the Hollywood cast-away and notorious bad girl Drew Barrymore.

Of course, Drew's reemergence as a star was not the result of any master plot on the part of the establishment. In fact, the transition happened quite by accident. In an inspired bit of casting, Drew finally landed her comeback role. The film was called *Poison Ivy*, and thanks to its unexpected success, Drew would never have to serve coffee again.

While Drew may not have been making big news in 1991, she was busy making movies. But make no mistake, Hollywood studios still shied away from the "disreputable" actress. Fortunately, independent film-makers were only too happy to pick up the slack. Not long after turning sixteen, Drew received a rather scandalous script from J. J. Harris, her agent. Although she didn't quite know what to make of the unscrupulous title character, Ivy, who befriends her classmate only to seduce her father and kill her mother, Drew did know that this was a role worth fighting for.

"Ivy was the kind of girl who in reality you would *never* want to become, but maybe when you were younger you even knew a girl like Ivy who made you say, 'Why can't I be that free? Why can't I just do the things she does, even though what she does is wrong? At least she has the guts to go and do it.' I loved Ivy so *much* for that and wanted to play her regardless of whether it was a good career move."

Drew's zest for the role, coupled with her wild past, was all it took to convince the directors that she was the only girl for the part. When she heard the news, Drew could hardly contain her glee. It had been so long since she'd last made a movie that she'd actually begun to wonder whether she was ever going to break through. Now, the dry spell was over and Drew was about to learn that when it rains, it pours.

Filming began in May 1991. Despite the long hours and the social isolation imposed by the stringent schedule, Drew came alive on the movie set just as she had in days of yore. Surrounded by a cast of consummate professionals such as lauded character actor Tom Skerritt (*A River Runs Through It*), former *Charlie's Angels'* Cheryl Ladd, and Sara Gilbert (*Roseanne*), Drew was back in her element and loving every minute of it.

Well, maybe every other minute. The film featured numerous love scenes between Drew and various other characters—actually, make that all the other characters. Drew was supposed to kiss both Sara Gilbert and Cheryl Ladd, as well as engage in a hot and heavy sex scene with fifty-eight-year-old Tom Skerritt. While the lesbian scenes didn't give Drew much pause, going at it with a man old enough to be her grandfather was something of a stretch even for this versatile young actress. "I was much more nervous kissing Tom than Sara," Drew admitted. "Tom, he's like this elderly man who, you know, is extremely conservative, and after a love scene with Tom we'd sort of like shake hands, hug, laugh a little bit, and walk in opposite directions. Whereas Sara and I were sort of giggly girls about it."

In time, even the role of Ivy would start to wear away at Drew's psyche. In the movie, Ivy is a new kid at school who's befriended by Sara Gilbert's lonely character Sylvie Cooper. In no time, Ivy worms her way into the good graces of the entire Cooper family, befriending Sylvie's ailing mother, played by Cheryl Ladd, and her wealthy father who is played by Tom Skerritt. Seeing that Sylvie's mom is suffering from emphysema, Ivy implements a systematic plot to take over her role in the household. While Drew may have envied Ivy's nerve at first reading, portraying such a thoroughly malevolent character on a daily basis proved a stressful experience. "It was really hard for me," she said. "I'm wicked in that movie. It was hard being Ivy for three months. I thought I would go insane. I'm a nice person. She's like the evilest woman in the world, and sometimes I felt like I was going crazy. Yeah, it was difficult because after a month I just wanted to be myself, but it was a great working experience, and it was because at the same time I loved being her."

When the film wrapped, Drew returned to her apartment and promptly learned that she was being considered for a whole series of movie roles. Still not in the enviable position to pick and choose, she was glad that at least one of the parts offered her was something that she could sink her teeth into. The movie was a made-for-Showtime feature called *Guncrazy,* and it promised to stretch Drew's acting muscle to the very limits of endurance by casting her in the role of a small-town floosie who falls head over heels for a convict and sets off on a wild crime spree à la *Bonnie and Clyde.*

"What was so amazing, was Drew called me personally," Tamra Davis, the film's director, revealed to the *E! True Hollywood Story.* "She called me on the phone while

I was casting . . . and she said 'This is Drew Barrymore, I read the script and you have to see me. I love this character more than anything. I *have* to play this character.' "

Davis agreed, and after one meeting, Drew had the role. "I drove home from the interview, like, totally in love with her, just madly in love with her, she completely bewitched me," Davis enthused.

Aside from *Guncrazy,* Drew also won a small but pivotal role in the Sean Young cable flick *Sketch Artist,* and a starring role as the fourteen-year-old central character in the wholly unremarkable B movie *No Place to Hide.* While the latter film was notable only for the chance it gave Drew to act opposite Kris Kristofferson, the part in *Sketch Artist* would prompt her to give one of her best performances as an adult actress and elicit rave reviews from the suddenly interested film community.

With all these films in the works, one would have expected Drew's personal life to suffer. Nothing could have been further from the truth. An industry veteran through and through, Drew had no trouble reacclimating to a lights-camera-action-packed schedule. In fact, only a few months after breaking up with Leland Hayward, Drew was back on the dating scene. But this, too, would soon pass.

As it turned out, J. J. Harris, Drew's agent, had been busy with much more than contract negotiations. Even as Drew was planning to live happily ever after with Hayward, J. J. was thinking about setting her up with one of her clients, an up-and-coming actor/musician named Jamie Walters.

Once Drew was free there was nothing to stop J. J.

from making her move. Still, the savvy agent bided her time. Looking to make a real match, and not a rebound relationship, she waited until Drew had sufficiently recovered from her broken engagement before introducing her to Jamie. "She was very smart," Drew stressed.

It was not until September '91 that Drew and Jamie finally had their first date. Since both were appropriately nervous and neither really expected to find true love at the outset, Drew and Jamie were shocked to discover that J. J. had been dead-on. The evening that was supposed to consist of little more than dinner and a movie stretched to nine hours. Walking down the Venice Beach promenade, Drew just kept thinking that she'd "never felt so comfortable and free with someone." Meanwhile, Jamie could hardly bring himself to take his eyes off of Drew. "What turned me on the most," he recalled, "is that she was there, looking me in the eye."

Discussing their life experiences, respective upbringings, and everything else under the California moon, the two "stayed up all night long," recounted Jamie, "sitting and talking." By sunrise, Drew and Jamie had become the best of friends. More important, they'd fallen in love.

For some time, the relationship would remain a well-kept secret. Indeed, the only thing that anyone knew about Drew's love life was what *People* magazine printed in its pages, namely that she'd recently written a fan letter to *90210*'s Jason Priestley.

Working either at her movie roles or at her relationships, Drew was always pressed for time. Her labors,

A star is born

A little princess

With mother, Jaid,
in front of the
Barrymore Theatre

Kidding around
with friend Amy
at the
Nickelodeon Kid's
Choice Awards

Success!
Drew at the
Women in
Hollywood gala

Stardom! Drew in
Batman Forever

Drew can cook

At the Sixth
Annual Celebrity
Server Dinner at
Palm Restaurant,
West Hollywood

∽Downtown girl∽

Steve Finn/Globe Photos

With Jamie Walters
at Cannes in 1992

Drew and

Lisa Rose/Globe Photos

With Luke Wilson at the
Premiere of *Ever After*

With Ed Norton at the 1999 Acadamy Awards

her leading men

With Dougray Scott from a scene in *Ever After*

Tom Green—
the man of her
dreams

however, were not for nothing. All would bear fruit the following year.

The romance was the first to mature. In February 1992, shortly after finishing *Guncrazy* and just as she was about to turn seventeen, Drew and Jamie took the plunge and moved in together. Aside from her three-month experience with David Crosby and Jan Dance, it was the first time in Drew's life that she had lived with a man, much less a boyfriend. She couldn't have been happier.

The relationship showed no signs of malaise after the pair decided to merge rental agreements. Pretty soon, the two were brainstorming an all-purpose pet name ("Bear-Bear"), setting up rules for their onscreen sex scenes with others ("no tongue—that's the first rule," explained Jamie, "and no real being naked."), tattooing each other's names on their backs, and generally driving their friends crazy in the process. "We're always trying to be as close as we can," Drew said. "And when we're with other people individually, all we do is talk about each other. So friends get frustrated."

The public had also been growing rather restless—the popular complaint, however, was not too much talk about Drew, but rather too little. The warm reception that greeted her latest dramatic efforts was proof positive of this overwhelming demand. The time was ripe for an all-out comeback, and Drew's agent was the first to hear about it. "Once people started seeing a little bit of footage from [*Poison Ivy*], J. J. got all these calls, like, 'We've got this role for Drew as a Lolitaesque nymphet,'" Drew explained. "And people were coming up to me on the set, going, 'How does it feel to be a sex symbol?' I was like, 'Me?!'"

Everything seemed to be coming together for Drew when *Poison Ivy* was released in May 1992. After its January premiere at the 1992 Sundance Film Festival in Park City, Utah, the movie had profited from good word-of-mouth and plenty of people were eager to see Drew bare down in the illicit thriller. Needless to say, they would not be disappointed. Although the film itself received a rather mixed bag of reviews, Drew was a hands-down favorite. *Entertainment Weekly* voiced the prevailing sentiment, raving that "Barrymore is a vivid presence" and that "her fresh-yet-jaded sultriness is alive on screen." Meanwhile, *Interview* magazine cheered that "That role . . . gained immeasurably from the actress's impersonation of sluggish sensuality and casual amorality."

To put it bluntly, Drew had indeed become a sex symbol. The magazines were once again interested, the fan base of lovestruck males was growing fast, and Drew was one of the most intriguing people of 1992—even if *People* magazine didn't come out and anoint her as such. The general population's opinion of Drew was that she was a wild child, and at a time when pop culture was experimenting with the dubious appeal of heroin chic, this was definitely a plus.

Of course, the public's image of Drew was hardly what anyone who knew her would have called on the money. In her comeback vehicle, *Poison Ivy,* Drew's costumes included cowboy boots, tight shirts, short skirts, and an abundance of ruby red lipstick. In real life, however, Drew was steeped in the flannel-shirt-ripped-jeans aesthetic that had come out of Seattle's alt rock scene.

It's no coincidence that Jamie Walters was also rarely

seen without his grunge fatigues, since Drew basically borrowed the fashion statement from her boyfriend. At the time of *Poison Ivy*'s release, the two love birds were just as crazy about each other as ever. Although the pair had been dating less than a year, their relationship was just like a marriage. They redecorated their West Hollywood apartment, owned a dog, and planned on moving into a bigger place with a yard. In May, the two even put in a joint appearance at the Cannes Film Festival.

While in France, the couple was disappointed to find that the festival was mostly about business. Networking, negotiating, schmoozing . . . they hated it. But when they tried to get away from all the madness by going shopping at Chanel, the slovenly dressed duo were promptly shown the door.

Shortly after returning from Cannes, Drew agreed to pose nude, albeit strategically positioned, on the cover of *Interview* magazine—but only if Jamie was allowed to be in the photo with her. For all intents and purposes, they were a couple. On June 20, 1992, they decided to go ahead and make it official: Jamie proposed, Drew said yes, and the month of May '93 was cleared for a wedding. "She was crying; I was charged," recounted Jamie. "It was really cool."

One reason that Drew and Jamie might have decided to get married so soon was the upward trajectory of their career paths. While Jamie had been wallowing in uncertainty when he first met Drew, the months they'd spent together had seen him catch the attention of one Aaron Spelling, television producer extraordinaire. Hired to star in *The Heights,* a *Beverly Hills 90210*-ish prime time drama, he was verging on stardom and seeking to follow in the footsteps of such crossovers as Johnny Depp and Luke Perry.

Jamie's decision to pursue a role in television may very well account for Drew's own rather uncharacteristic move onto the small screen. Just as her boyfriend was signing his contract for FOX's *The Heights,* Drew was auditioning for CBS's *2000 Malibu Road,* yet another Aaron Spelling production modeled after the *90210* prototype. Besides a star-studded cast that included Jennifer Beals and Lisa Hartman, the series also boasted the directorial skills of Joel Schumacher. But, despite her admiration for Schumacher, whom she first met while club-hopping with her mom at the tender age of eight, Drew remained apprehensive. Films were still her first love and she didn't want to wake up five years down the line only to find that she'd been pigeonholed as a TV actress. "I was closed off to the idea of TV until Joel Schumacher started telling me about *2000 Malibu Road* and I read the first two episodes."

Impressed with her character's development as well as with the show's never-ending twists and turns, Drew put her worries aside and signed on the dotted line. She would play a timid young actress who comes to the West Coast with her manager/sister. As the plot unfolds, the character overcomes seemingly insurmountable odds to become a self-assured superstar. "I like transitions," said Drew, "and my character in the show starts scared and then becomes very strong—women aren't usually written that way."

Although *The Heights* was filmed in Vancouver and *2000 Malibu Road* in California, the distance did not seem to bother the lovestruck pair at first. Drew and Jamie were having far too much fun relishing the unexpected turns of their careers to worry about any impending "out of sight, out of mind" relationship difficulties. While Drew was working on the series, for instance, *Poison Ivy* had debuted as well as Showtime's *Sketch Artist*. While the former film won her the undying admiration of the Gen-X set, the latter netted her a heaping helping of great reviews. According to *The Record*'s TV critic, Virginia Mann, *Sketch Artist*'s "most impressive cast member is Barrymore, who manages to make her character distinctive and believable before Daisy disappears from the film—far too soon."

Now, there was no denying that Drew had effected a total comeback. But even as everyone was rooting for her continued success, the actress was feeling a bit overwhelmed by all the attention. Her phone never stopped ringing, the tabloids were once again hot on her trail, and the scripts piled up by the dozens. Of course, having been through the publicity avalanche before, Drew's attitude towards the hoopla was a great deal more tempered. "Everybody's all over me," she couldn't help saying, "but I know that next month the hype might not be there."

To capitalize upon her newfound popularity, Drew resolved to pack as much work as possible into her schedule. Since Jamie was busy shooting and promoting *The Heights*, Drew had plenty of time to go out on auditions and promote her own forthcoming series. CBS had picked up *2000 Malibu Road* for a trial run of five weeks. The production costs for the series were an astronomical $1.3 million per episode. Even Aaron Spelling had to admit that it was one of "the most expensive shows we have ever produced." With such a steep price tag the show would have to deliver equally substantial ratings to stay on the air, and the network figured that five weeks was just enough time to gauge the public's response.

As it turned out, five weeks was all the airtime that *2000 Malibu Road* would get to see. Although the ratings for the August '92 series were actually quite high, they did not manage to offset the exorbitant production costs and CBS passed on the series. This was a lucky break for Drew. The show had given her mass exposure as well as the chance to work with Joel Schumacher, and all this with no commitment. Having had her cake and eaten it, too, Drew was relieved to continue on with her thriving film career.

The buzz surrounding the new and improved Drew Barrymore was growing more deafening by the day, and the October '92 debut of *Guncrazy* only served to pump up the volume on the hype meter. Singled out for her performance, Drew found herself back at the center of media scrutiny as a Golden Globe best actress nominee. "I was shocked when I was nominated," Drew effused. "It's a real honor and much of the credit goes to Tamra because she's easily the best director I've ever worked with. Anyone who gets to work with her is lucky because the scope of her talent is huge and her vision is really pure."

Much more than a mere honor, the nomination signaled Drew's admission back into the Hollywood fold.

No longer beyond the pale, she was once again a highly sought after star, and she had the film offers to prove it.

Jamie was also riding high on a wave of tremendous success. While his series had hit the skids after nary a season, his musical aspirations were finally coming to fruition. In fact, according to the *Billboard Hot 100,* Jamie's was the Number One song in the country. "How Do You Talk to an Angel" came directly off *The Heights* soundtrack, and with Jamie playing guitar and singing lead vocal, his star was shining just as bright as his fiancée's.

As hard as she tried to give Jamie her full and undivided attention, Drew simply couldn't afford to turn down lucrative job offers. Jamie was also in no position to look down his nose at well-paying gigs. At this stage of their lives, the couple's careers demanded every last ounce of their energy. Hoping that their relationship could survive on love alone, each had to be content with taking whatever the other had left to give—which wasn't much, considering their respective professional obligations.

What finally brought the love affair to a screeching halt was neither familial meddling (Jaid approved of the match) nor irreconcilable differences (Jamie and Drew agreed on nearly everything). Rather it was the making of *The Amy Fisher Story* that did the relationship in once and for all. Although there had already been signs of trouble in Drew and Jamie's paradise, the frantic, three-week shoot in Vancouver seemed to come as something of a last straw. As Drew explained, "I've never cared about another human being before like I cared about Jamie, but the amount of time we had to spend apart completely took its toll on us. We never saw each other, and things got worse and worse."

Certainly, Drew cannot be faulted for accepting the role of Amy "The Long Island Lolita" Fisher and the challenge that it represented. She knew she had to do it just as surely as she knew that she was far too old to ever reprise the role of the original Lolita. This was her chance to portray a real-life woman, and she meant to do the role justice.

The sordid incident upon which the movie was based had rocked the nation in the spring of 1992. By the onset of fall, there were an unprecedented three television movies—all dealing with the same subject matter and scheduled for concurrent broadcast—already in the works. It was the kind of true crime story that seemed custom-made for television. Seventeen-year-old Amy Fisher had shown up at the Long Island home of Mary Jo Buttafuoco. When Mary Jo answered the door, Fisher shot her in the head, leaving her alive but crippled with partial facial paralysis. The motive for Amy Fisher's actions? An affair with Mary Jo's thirty-eight-year-old husband, Joey Buttafuoco. Fisher's history as a call girl, Joey's vehement denial of his all-too-real no-tell motel trysts with the teenager, and Mary Jo's insistence on standing by her man all combined to make the "Long Island Lolita" scandal the hottest, most compelling property to hit the media in years. Even Drew had been drawn in by the salacious headlines. "I remember when this story came out, talking to my friends, saying, 'I can't believe she [Fisher] actually did that.' "

Six months later, NBC, CBS, and ABC were all scrambling to bring their Amy Fisher movies to television. CBS had the rights to the Buttafuocos' story and NBC had snagged the Amy Fisher testimony. Meanwhile, ABC's sole bid for legitimacy was Drew Barrymore, a major motion picture star and herself no stranger to scandal and controversy.

Fully aware that hopes for the film's ratings rested squarely on her shoulders, Drew focused all of her energy on preparing for the role. Despite the similarities between Amy Fisher and her other "Lethal Lolita" characters in *Poison Ivy* and *Guncrazy*, Drew had no intention of ascribing any fictional qualities to her very real role. After all, just because Amy emerged as a caricature in the press didn't mean that Drew had to commit the same errors of oversimplification. She was going to make her Amy believable if it was the last thing she ever did.

For Drew, the hard part wasn't relating to Amy the obsessed teen, but to Amy the gun-toting killer. The actress had had her share of failed romances and simulating a spurned lover for the cameras was the least of her difficulties. The part where Amy pulls the trigger, however, was not anything that Drew could so much as begin to understand. "This kind of story usually takes place with adults. But this one involved a young girl," she explained. "Of course, someone my age would wonder how in the hell—why in the hell—someone would do something like this. . . . This girl actually went out and shot this woman."

Thinking back to her own brushes with physical violence must have helped Drew execute the critical front door scene in which Amy shoots Mary Jo. But while drawing on her own experience aided her performance, the exercise did nothing for her ability to comprehend Fisher's criminal actions. Drew did what she could to bring authenticity to the role by nailing Amy Fisher's unique Long Island accent. "It's amazing," she marveled to *Newsday*. "There are like fifty dialects from Long Island and I had to study the one from her particular part. There must be five different groups of 'A's' there. There's the typical 'Awww' 'A,' and then there's the 'eh' 'A,' like in marriage."

Somehow, Drew managed to pick up the accent in time. By the November 23 start of the three-week, sixteen-hour-per-day shoot, she talked, walked, and—with the help of a wig—even looked like Amy Fisher. The transformation was truly remarkable. And as the huge audiences would soon confirm, of the three actresses who portrayed the Long Island Lolita, Drew was far and away the best.

No doubt, it was the thespian's compassion for her subject's plight that enabled her to deliver such a moving performance. Throughout the filming, Drew could feel Amy's pain just by noticing that her own boyfriend was growing increasingly distant. Although she tried to keep her mind on her work, the problems in her relationship became impossible to ignore when Jamie called her on December 13, 1992, just three days prior to her return. Although tempered with love, his message was loud and clear—he was moving out and their engagement was off.

Drew asked Jamie to wait until she got back so they

could talk through their issues in person, but her supplications fell on deaf ears. By the time she got back, he was gone.

A Golden Globe nomination, a universally acclaimed TV movie that swept the Nielsens, and a future full of promise—it should have been the happiest time of Drew's life. Instead, she was making herself miserable by desperately trying to keep her relationship with Jamie from falling apart. Although he'd moved out of their home, the two kept on dating in the hope of salvaging the romance. "Jamie and I are separated," she sadly confessed to *Cosmopolitan,* "and we're trying to work on it. The one thing that we have going for us, one of our strongest points, is we're the best of friends . . . As hard as it is being separated, at the same time I have hope for the future for us, and if not, I know that we'll always be in each other's lives."

With the house to herself, Drew made haste to find a roommate. Her best friend of some years, Justine Baddeley, fit the bill perfectly. As it happened, twenty-nine-year-old Justine was also going through some heartbreak of her own, and the two friends leaned on each other for support. "I live with Justine, and we watch movies or go out to the movies, or . . . my favorite time, when my friends come over and we cook," Drew said in May of 1993. "I read, I paint, I write. My lifestyle is very un-Hollywood."

But if Drew and Jamie thought that more time apart was the answer to their romantic woes, they'd soon find out they were wrong. As so often happens, a trial separation was but the beginning of the end, and when Drew realized as much she said, "I've never felt pain like this in my entire life." She forgot all about her once passionate feelings for Leland Hayward, claiming that she'd "never been in love before except for Jamie. I don't even know if I could be in love again after him."

If Drew's statements of lovers torn asunder sound too tragic to swallow, perhaps it's because the pain was still fresh in her memory when she made them. Some two years later, a more clear-headed Jamie would look back and put the relationship into perspective. "That relationship got so much attention," he'd comment, "and I'm not exactly sure why. It didn't last that long. She and I are still friends. The time wasn't right to get that serious with each other."

Sure enough, Drew would eventually get back into circulation. With her career on fast-forward and her independence reinstated, she burned all of the flannels that symbolically bound her to Jamie's Gen-X scene and "started to dress like a girl again." Although the grunge look was still all the rage in 1993, for Drew that phase had passed. Her days of playing teenage femme fatales in B movies and independent films were also history. Although her box office drawing power had yet to be proven, Hollywood was willing to roll the dice and take a chance on the starlet suddenly in demand. In the spirit of gambling, Drew would also throw caution to the wind and impetuously change her hard-won Killer Queen image into that of a playful wild child.

SEVEN

Wild Thing

If Drew knew only one thing about where she wanted to go with her career it was that she was sick and tired of playing "nymphets." Conscious of type-casting, she began to turn down scripts that so much as hinted of sexploitation, saying that "I'm grateful to have the opportunity to be selective, and I'm going to choose wisely."

Unfortunately, the powers that be had different ideas. As if determined to keep Drew in Catholic schoolgirl uniforms and lollipops, producers kept right on sending naughty-girl roles in her direction. "I think after *Poison Ivy* and *Guncrazy* and playing Amy Fisher, I did get all these bad-girl scripts," Drew mused, "and I was like, 'Well, that's nice, that you think that I do that well, that's a compliment in itself. But it's not the only thing I can do, and it's not the only thing I want to do.'"

Evading the torrent of offers to play bad girls, how-ever, would not be nearly so easy. Drew would have to wait months for the right script to come along. Luckily, she had the wherewithal to make good use of her down-time, signing up for a coveted cameo role in *Wayne's*

World 2 and, most surprising, agreeing to lend her face and form to an even more coveted modeling contract.

Georges Marciano's scintillating Guess? jeans ad campaigns had been making supermodels out of mere wanna-bes for some years by the time Drew was approached to pose in the summer of 1993. Claudia Schiffer had been the first and foremost Guess? girl; on her heels came the striking Carré Otis and the buxom Anna Nicole Smith. For the five foot four inch, ninety-eight pound Drew Barrymore of 1993, these amazonian women looked to be a tough act to follow—even if she *had* almost bared it all on the cover of *Interview* magazine just one year prior. "When my publicist called and said [Guess?] wanted me, I freaked," she revealed to *Entertainment Weekly*. "The other models are like six feet tall, drop-dead beautiful. People are going to look at my ass and go, 'Why did they do this?' "

The reason, of course, was that Drew had grown into an icon of sex appeal for her generation, and she'd done it without the aid of so much as one box office smash. The fact that her movies were cult faves rather than mainstream standards only added to Drew's allure. She wasn't Julia Roberts, she was cutting edge, and that in itself was compelling. Teens and twentysomethings alike were fixated on, fascinated by, and interested in Drew, and since Guess? jeans catered to this very demographic, Drew made for an ideal poster girl.

For her part, Drew had plenty of reasons to accept the offer, not the least of which was good, old-fashioned vanity. Although she'd rejected previous proposals from Gap, Pepe Jeans, and Capezio, the offer from the high profile and well-regarded Guess? campaign was, to use Drew's expression, "a dream come true." Still, when it came to her qualifications for the assignment, she had a hard time understanding what all the fuss was about. While the actress's many charms may have been obvious to the general public, they were lost on the naturally modest Drew. "It's so hard for me to look at myself, and think, 'Yeah, I'm sexy, I've got it going on.'" She shrugged.

To compound her confusion, the would-be model was feeling less fetching than ever the day that she first met Wayne Maser, the photographer in charge of the Guess? layout. An allergic reaction to an unidentified substance had left her skin covered with blotches. According to Drew, she looked "like a puffer fish that has acne or something."

No matter, Maser's expert eye saw right past the redness and the swelling. Drew was perfect. A weeklong Miami photo shoot was arranged for July, and Drew was officially anointed as the newest Guess? Girl.

While the provocative photos wouldn't hit magazines until October 1993, the actress had much to keep her occupied in the meantime. Her old friend and Guncrazy director, Tamra Davis, was helming another flick and Drew was again being featured front and center. Unlike Guncrazy, however, this particular movie came complete with a substantial budget and a cast of all-stars. In Bad Girls, Drew would be starring alongside such talents as Andie MacDowell, Madeleine Stowe, and Mary Stuart Masterson.

No two ways about it, this job was a big deal, heralding bigger and better things for Drew's career. Hard as she'd tried to stay away from so-called "bad girl" roles, the feminist Western with the acclaimed cast would bring Drew her first big budget studio picture in over six years. Although she'd spent the past two years toiling away in and making the best of Indie films, Drew knew all along that having her name listed next to those of her three *Bad Girls* costars would bring her that much closer to where she truly wanted to be—the A-list.

Just as the public's interest in Drew was reaching a near fever pitch, the actress's personal life was in a state of disrepair. Still smarting from her breakup with Jamie Walters, Drew was also overcome with some strong negative emotions toward her mom. Although the two didn't live together, their respective residences were only two blocks away from each other. With Jamie out of the picture, old mother-daughter patterns seemed to reemerge, and Drew didn't like the direction in which the relationship was heading.

Her business sense, on the other hand, was growing sounder by the day. In 1992, Drew had taken the first step toward what would one day become one of the most successful actor-run production companies in Hollywood: she hired Kim Greitzer as her own personal assistant. Initially, Kim just helped to keep Drew's then-humble affairs organized. Drew told *Interview* magazine in 1995 that their business relationship morphed into something bigger and better. "We worked together every day and really got to know each other, and it was like this amalgamation of two spirits. We learned that we both wanted the same things in life. We wanted to work hard and we didn't want our sex or our age ever to be held against us. We just wanted to, like, go forth with our dream. And our dream was to have a production company."

As the months sped by, the role of assistant began to expand into that of publicist, manager, and eventually business partner. Although Drew had yet to earn the industry's full trust, Kim's support helped her visualize the future. And with the *Bad Girls* role in the hopper, Drew's long-term goals of A-list stardom and her own production credits finally seemed to be within reach. After nearly twenty years in the business, Drew was at long last beginning to think like a true Hollywood insider. "Information is always your best asset," she stated, "to know what's going on, to be not only on top of the game but ahead of it. I learned I didn't want to sit back and wait for things to come to me. I wanted to create work for myself."

Feeling thoroughly empowered by her professional successes, Drew rebelled against accepting the escalating tensions between herself and Jaid. It was time to start calling the shots, and the Texas-based *Bad Girls* shoot gave Drew the chance to get out of Hollywood, clear her head, and think about her own well-being for five straight months. "My mom. We're like oil and water, we just don't mix," she explained shortly before *Bad Girls'* 1994 release. "I had been living the hardness of the lessons and not getting any knowledge from them, you know? I was alone for five months and, thank God, it started to pour. It was like a rain shower, the knowledge was just, like, flowing almost too fast to understand it. I had to escape and see everything very clearly to come into that."

This initial breach of contact would turn into a rift spanning years. According to Drew, there was just no common ground to be found—she hated the whole Hollywood scene and her mom loved it. Whatever problems this difference of opinion caused within the Barrymore women's relationship, they were apparently too serious to surmount. "I don't understand her," Drew related. "And I tried to for so long. I just think that too much shit has happened. I think we differ in the fact that she seems to love Hollywood and I hate Hollywood. It's a shallow, inconsistent, competitive, cruel world."

After taking about all she could handle of Tinseltown's often treacherous ways, Drew got another dose of the industry's fickle nature on the set of *Bad Girls*. With a ready script, an assembled cast, and a gung ho director in the person of Tamra Davis all raring to go, the shoot should have gone off without a hitch. Unfortunately, two weeks into the production, the company behind *Bad Girls* scrapped the script, let go of the director, and sent the principal actors off to cowboy boot camp while new writers and a new director were brought on board. Watching her friend Tamra Davis get the full Hollywood treatment couldn't have been easy for Drew, and the experience no doubt served to reinforce her worst suspicions about the seamier side of show business.

The revamped screenplay revolved around four prostitutes, Cody (Stowe), Anita (Masterson), Eileen (Mac-

Dowell), and Lilly (Barrymore) in the Wild Old West. After Cody kills a client who got too carried away at their brothel, she is sentenced to death by the local detective and the mob of townspeople. To save their friend, Anita, Eileen, and Lilly must join her in a life on the lam. Horseback-riding action and pistol-packing adventures ensue.

The hackneyed plot and uninspired direction were alone responsible for the film's underwhelming performance at the box office. The critics did not miss a beat, attributing their general displeasure to the movie rather than to its fine cast of actors. As Roger Ebert of the *Chicago Sun-Times* wrote, "the failure of *Bad Girls* is all the more poignant because the actresses are at the top of their forms right now, and could have been inspired by a more ambitious production."

Although the film fell flat with most audiences when it premiered in April 1994, Drew had far too much going on in her life at the time to worry about anything as trivial as other people's profits. Of course, had *Bad Girls* done tremendous box office the success would have been a boon for Drew's future paychecks. But then again, Drew had never been in the business for the money. Her dream was to act, to contribute, and to be recognized for so doing. And in April '94, as she worked to bring her character in *Boys on the Side* to life, this was one dream that Drew was actually living.

One mainstream film was all Drew had needed to break out of the small time. Suddenly, the young actress found herself besieged, movie offers were coming in from all sides. She was so delighted she had to laugh, literally. Drew's spirits were on a permanent high. She turned into a chronic giggler. She downed macaroni and cheese with absolute abandon. Thanks perhaps to her two-pack a day cigarette habit, she consumed mass quantities of the cheesy Kraft concotion without ever gaining so much as a pound.

For all appearances, Drew was on the manic ride of her life. She complained about insomnia, behaved impulsively, jump-started her production company, Flower Films, with Kim Greitzer, and worked on both sides of the camera. Something about the *Bad Girls* shoot must have set her off, because when Drew returned to Hollywood, she was a new and unabashedly wild woman. For a long time, she'd had to struggle to prove her sobriety, maturity, and professionalism to a skeptical industry convinced that she was a drug addict. It was almost as if the role in *Bad Girls,* and the prestigious job offers that quickly followed, had come as some sort of an assurance, a guarantee that she was once again a big star and could at last let go and have some fun.

Toward that end, Drew's first order of business after signing on to star in *Boys on the Side* was to go off the deep end. Taking the biggest plunge of all, Drew exchanged marital vows with her beau of five weeks in March '94. Whether the marriage was a calculated publicity stunt or the impetuous act of free spirit is still uncertain, but Drew did grace Jay Leno's *Tonight Show* couch the very next week to discuss the romantic ceremony, as well as to promote the upcoming release of *Bad Girls.* The ratings for that night's show were some of the highest Jay had ever seen. Everyone, it seems, was dying to hear about Drew's crazy, spur-of-the-moment wedding.

The lucky groom was Jeremy Thomas, a British seaman turned L.A. bar owner. Drew had known him for two years before she started dating him in February '94. At 2:00 A.M. on March 20, 1994, the two were making time together when Drew popped the question. "Actually we had been discussing it together for a couple of weeks!" she explained. "It kept going back and forth and after a while it was, 'Why bicker about it? Let's just do it and see what happens.'"

The wacky couple promptly called 1-800-I-MARRY-YOU and were immediately set up with a female psychic priest who agreed to perform the ceremony. A few hours later Drew Barrymore, clad in a white slip dress and combat boots, was standing in the basement of her fiancé's bar, The Room, and saying "I do" in the presence of a few of her nearest and dearest.

Soon after the wedding, Drew went on record with her marital bliss. "I have someone else I have to think about in the world," she gushed. "I have another half, you know? Which I love! I love this person! And it means being completely selfless, which is a very grounding thing . . . I always wanna be aware of what I have and never forget that and never not be grateful for it. And that's not just with my marriage, that's with everything."

Five days into the union, Drew set off for Tucson, Arizona, to film *Boys on the Side* and not to see her husband again until, well, until the inevitable divorce. The marriage lasted a grand total of six weeks, four and a half of which Drew spent on location. "I think we would have been married for about one minute if I hadn't been," she said after the bitter divorce. "I hate him so much."

According to Drew's post breakup testimony, she'd only married Thomas to help him get a green card. His true colors, however, only revealed themselves after the quickie ceremony. "He turned out to be the biggest schmuck I've ever met in all my years of existence," Drew railed. "He gained everything. I got nothing out of it, except to look like the world's biggest asshole . . . It was a green card situation. That's why I couldn't tell anybody."

During the divorce, Thomas apparently tried to get his hands on some of Drew's hard-earned money. But Drew wasn't budging, saying that "He can't have anything of mine. He couldn't even have my toenail." Meanwhile, the spectators of the world looked on, heads a'shaking, tongues a'clicking, tsk, tsk, tsk, these Hollywood people and their marriages. All the speculation had Drew steaming mad. "It was more personal than a book," she said. "Having the whole world judge you for a mistake that many human beings make in this world but don't necessarily have the public scrutiny of millions and millions of people all over the world."

The truth was that Drew Barrymore didn't need anyone to wag their finger and chastise her. She knew full well that she'd screwed up royally. "It's the only thing I've ever done in my life that was untruthful to myself," she stated. "It's really ruined marriage for me."

Sure enough, Drew has remained a swinging single ever since the Jeremy Thomas debacle. Although she might have gotten married any number of times, she learned her lesson the hard way and wouldn't make the same mistake twice.

Thanks to the role of Holly Gooding in *Boys on the Side*, Drew was able to bounce right back from her divorce disaster. The character drew upon the most positive aspects of her personality and brought out her natural joie de vivre. "Holly's definitely different from any of the characters I've played," she explained. "She's not dramatic. She's funny and light and spirited. Holly's like this flower and you see her open up and blossom and metamorphose, which is really cool. . . . The truth of the matter is, I am the silliest person on the planet. I am really, really goofy. And it was so great for me to put my goofiness to productive use through Holly. I left every day with this simple, light, beautiful feeling."

In the movie, Whoopi Goldberg plays Jane, a lounge singer who is fed up with New York. In need of a traveling companion, she hits upon Mary-Louise Parker's character, Robin, a real estate broker who is also looking to escape the rat race. The two women set off on a road trip, stopping only to pick up Holly, who is being abused by her drug-dealing boyfriend. Suffice it to say that *Boys on the Side* is a tearjerker with a bright side named Drew Barrymore. Although the film touches on some mighty heavy issues, Drew's character endowed it with a much-needed dose of fun.

Working with *Boys on the Side* director Herbert Ross

as well as her costars Whoopi Goldberg, Mary-Louise Parker, and Matthew McConaughey also contributed to Drew's happy state of mind. Although she had much to brood over, including her divorce, her claustrophobia-induced attacks of anxiety, and the disappointing performance of the recently released *Bad Girls,* the supportive vibe on the movie set carried Drew through the many long, lonely nights that she spent at her luxurious Tucson hotel room. Of course, no one could help her when time came to turn out the lights—not even her character Holly.

But while the role might have been of no use to Drew the insomniac, it was instrumental for Drew the actress. Herbert Ross, for one, couldn't have been more pleased with the uniquely insightful performance delivered by Drew. After the shoot was complete, Ross had free rein to rave about the young actress. "Drew recognized something in the role that hadn't been tapped before," he enthused. "There was humor, wit and bravery—in addition to sweetness and goodness—all of which exist in Drew. I had no idea she was an actress of the quality she is. I think this picture has done her a great deal of good. She'll be taken seriously now."

Ross's prediction was right on target. Despite Drew's nude scene—rarely a good idea for a "serious" American actress—the movie's February '95 release would bring her some of the best reviews of her career. Referring to Drew as the "catalyst of the group," Roger Ebert wrote that "those who know Barrymore from her adolescent headlines in the supermarket trash press may not realize that in movies like *Guncrazy* (1992), she has been developing into an actress of great natural zest and conviction."

Other film critics were quick to agree with Ebert's assessment. The *San Francisco Chronicle*'s Mick LaSalle sang Drew's praises, calling her "about the closest thing to Jean Harlow since Jean Harlow. With fine comic finesse she plays Holly, a free spirit who joins the cross-country trip following a brawl with her drug-dealing boyfriend." The *Washington Post*'s Rita Kempley, meanwhile, likened Drew to Carole Lombard, observing that she "brings something new to the screen."

All told, the release of *Boys on the Side* would net Drew a world of credibility, affirming that her Golden Globe nominated performance in *Guncrazy* wasn't so much a fluke as a sign of things to come.

After completing her work on *Boys on the Side,* Drew didn't wait around to see how the film community would react. Instead she got right back into the swing of things in Los Angeles. Much as Drew affected to dislike the entertainment industry, there was no denying that that was where she felt most at home. Lending credence to her claim that "whenever I get sad that I'm involved in [show business], I feel that instead of sitting on the sidelines and complaining I should go in there and make it better," she made room in her busy schedule to officially start up her own production company, Flower Films, with Kim Greitzer.

"It's two girlies wanting to make good movies, with people who are passionate," Drew later explained, "and I never thought that I would be into this side of the business, but I've found myself really into it. . . . We're very much on the same wavelength in a business sense. We sit down with, like, our iced teas and cigarettes at our desk and we just plow through the day. We do it together, and it's really great. Not every decision has to have the weight of the world on it. Then again, certain decisions do. And that is why Kim and I will probably have ulcers in the next ten years. But there's nothing that snakes by us, you know?"

It certainly appeared as if Drew was right, at least when it came to her own movie roles. Whereas Flower Films was still in its infancy, Drew's movie career was soaring into the stratosphere. The actress only had a few precious days to enjoy the comfort of her SoCal home before her presence was again needed on yet another shoot location, this time in Seattle.

In *Mad Love,* she'd be playing Casey, a bipolar teen who moves to Seattle and sweeps costar Chris O'Donnell's character, Matt, off his feet. Getting cast opposite one of America's teen dreams was proof of Hollywood's full faith in Drew's crowd-pleasing abilities. Her previous big-budget features, *Bad Girls* and *Boys on the Side,* had both been ensemble pieces and neither had performed all that well at the box office. But with *Mad Love,* Drew was finally being given her chance to shine.

Ever the consummate actress, Drew was quick to analyze her role and come to an understanding of her character's development. "I think the best way I can describe Casey is that she's a late-blooming little flower," Drew mused. "She has a terrible time, and it isn't understood why until it's realized that she's manic-depressive. Her behavior starts to deteriorate in the midst of her first experience of love, and she desperately tries to grasp reality as she's falling deeper and deeper into the ether of her mind."

Clearly, here was a role to which Drew could relate wholeheartedly. Much like Casey, Drew knew only too well how it felt to be confined to an institution. Her character's flight from authority was also something with which she'd had firsthand experience. She had only to recall her thirteenth summer, when she stole her now-estranged mother's credit card and flew clear across the country with her friend, to understand Casey's motivation for running away from home. Sensing that she could play this role blindfolded, Drew had no problem convincing the casting directors that she was the woman for the job.

Despite the attendant trauma of reliving her painful experiences as an addict/alcoholic, bringing the role of Casey to life proved to be highly therapeutic. "To be in that mentality constantly for three months—I must say, it drove me nuts," she confessed. "It killed my spirit to play this character. But when it was over, the cathartic aspect of it kicked in, and I felt freer than I've ever felt. To go through all that and come out the other side is a revelation in the highest sense—without question."

Drew's facility with the character gave her performance an air of confidence that was not lost on her costar. Watching Drew in action gave Chris O'Donnell chills. In fact, like so many people meeting Drew for the first time, he couldn't believe that she was only nineteen years old. "Drew is not self-conscious at all. She's very sure of herself—opinionated, even," he said. "She doesn't sit and think about things. She knows what she likes and where she wants to go with her character. That makes her seem much older than she is." The two costars got along famously.

The guy who'd be the true love of Drew's life had already arrived—some four months earlier. That first chance meeting had gone down at a noisy Seattle nightclub where a group called That Dog was playing. Drew had been invited to attend by That Dog's front woman, her friend, Anna Waronker. Guitarist Eric Erlandson of Courtney Love's band Hole was also on the guest list— as Drew quickly found out for herself.

As if to prove that love truly does conquer all, Eric and Drew met when a nasty case of food poisoning caused her to spew her undigested macaroni and cheese all over his shoes. "It was so embarrassing," Drew shuddered. "He said, 'Honestly, this is what everybody in the world does at one point. I'd appreciate it if you'd let me stay with you.' And I was like, 'Wow. Who are you? You are amazing.' So we sat there and we talked for a while, and he made me laugh."

Much as Drew enjoyed her evening with Eric, the two parted company as friends and nothing more. Neither had so much as an inkling that they were destined to fall in love. Then Drew came knocking on Eric's hotel room door two weeks later. According to Drew, photographer Ellen von Unworth had mistakenly given her the wrong room number. She had no idea it was Eric's room until he opened the door and said, "Oh, my God, macaroni and cheese." Taken completely off guard,

Drew could only think of one thing to do. "I grabbed him and gave him this huge kiss." Oddly enough, it would take yet a third such encounter for the rock star and movie star to realize that they were indeed star-crossed lovers. This time, Drew was in Seattle to shoot *Mad Love*. More than four months had passed since her last interlude with Eric, and yet she still had no problem identifying the voice that whispered, "Have you eaten any macaroni and cheese lately?" into her ear just one week after she arrived on location. "And there he was," Drew recalled nearly a year later. "And we've been together ever since."

What with working on two major motion pictures back to back, how Drew ever found time for romance was anybody's guess. Besides *Mad Love*, Drew spent the summer of '94 filming Joel Schumacher's *Batman Forever*, starring Val Kilmer, Nicole Kidman, Jim Carrey, Tommy Lee Jones, and Drew's newfound bud Chris O'Donnell. But while Drew's daily planner defied all reason, the young actress wouldn't have had it any other way. For someone who'd been unable to so much as get arrested in Hollywood just four short years before, the opportunity to play a role in a summer blockbuster was mind-blowing—even if that role didn't amount to much more than a cameo. But lest anyone think that Drew stood in danger of getting tripped up by the glare of the spotlight, she never failed to remind herself how far she'd once fallen, how far she'd come, and how far she still had left to go. "The truth is," she explained, "I know it can all fucking go away again in a heartbeat. That's why I will always be grateful for every job I get."

For the role of Sugar in *Batman Forever,* Drew felt she owed her gratitude to her old friend and her greatest champion Joel Schumacher, who had actually suggested her for *2000 Malibu Road.* "He was there for me always," Drew expressed. "He's always been a strong, supportive friend to me."

Schumacher's good deeds on Drew's behalf, however, were not all selfless. After all, as a director he did have a little something to gain from an actress of Drew's caliber. "I think Drew is one of the most honest actors I've ever worked with," he said. "With Drew, what you see is what you get. When the cameras are rolling, she starts speaking and you almost think she didn't hear 'action.' It sounds like a conversation, not like acting. . . . There is a luminous quality to Drew's skin and eyes. The camera just loves her, and it has all her life—it's a God-given gift."

As always, Drew gave as good as she got. Upon *Batman Forever*'s summer '95 release, she did all she could to bolster the film's chances, even though she wasn't technically a principal actor. She even went on record to state, "I won't say it's better than the other Batman films 'cause that can be misconstrued as snotty, but I think it's very different from the others. It has a genius screenplay that takes you into this realm of total imagination, and I love the fact that Joel played that up. He really went for the comic-strip idea and the surrealism of that."

Thanks to Schumacher's faith in her acting abilities, and the movie's warm and lovable cast of characters, Drew had had a blast on the set of *Batman Forever*. She dressed up in glitter, modeled herself after Marilyn Monroe, and generally camped it up playing sweet sugar against Debi Mazar's naughty spice. However, the experience wasn't nearly as much fun as Val Kilmer's ex-wife Joanne Whalley might have thought when she named Drew as one of Kilmer's extramarital affairs in divorce court. Drew's response to the accusation made clear that she and Kilmer were just good friends. The same could not be said for the notoriously difficult Kilmer and Joel Schumacher, who did nothing except butt heads for the duration of the *Batman* shoot.

Certainly, Drew's rantings about her love for Eric gave no indication that she would ever stray into another's arms. You didn't have to be Freud to figure out that these were the words of a woman in love: "He's the most beautiful soul I've ever come across. I'm the luckiest girl in the world to be with him and I know it."

The relationship threw Drew into a rock 'n' roll fantasy world. She attended Eric's concerts, visited him in the recording studio, and was a constant presence both backstage and at Hole's various parties. But the partying wasn't always so smooth, especially when Drew was first introduced to the larger-than-life persona of Courtney Love. "There was tension in the beginning," Drew later admitted.

At the time, however, she made the best of Courtney Love's somewhat aloof attitude, telling one interviewer that "As much as I'm around that scene, I'm very rarely around her. I feel like I relate to this person so much, and yet in other ways we seem so opposite. But then I think that we're the kind of people who don't feel like we need to try and be best friends. We just don't mind each other's presence, and sometimes I respect that as much as I do friendship."

In any case, Drew had way too much going on in her own life to concern herself with matters as trivial as who might or might not like her. Aside from her relationship with Eric, she still had her acting, her production company, and now that she was done with *Mad Love,* her therapy sessions. Drew hadn't been in group therapy or on a psychologist's couch since she was fifteen. She hated the rules that went along with organizations such as Alcoholics Anonymous, found psychoanalysis far too self-indulgent, and generally fared much better on her own. But her grueling role in *Mad Love* had really gotten to her, bringing up a mixed bag of issues that Drew felt she needed to address with a therapist.

Drew's Flower Films was also in constant need of attention. As she was not content to be a producer in name only, she wanted to ferret out projects, find financing, and basically tackle every behind-the-scenes aspect of this stress-inducing job. And now that her mad shooting spree—in *Boys on the Side, Mad Love,* and *Batman Forever*—had run its course, Drew renewed her commitment to the business of Flower Films. "Everyone wants that producer plaque on their door, but it takes an extraordinary amount of work to get there," Drew said. "It takes education and research and really going to the college of film and production."

Enter Nancy Juvonen. At the start of 1994, Nancy's brother introduced her to Drew. Less than two weeks later, Drew called Nancy at her San Francisco home and offered her a job with Flower Films. Moving to Los Angeles, however, was not the only catch; since Drew was by no means convinced of Nancy's qualifications, the rookie would have to pay her dues. "The first three months was getting groceries, picking out tiles, redoing her house, and cleaning the pool." Nancy groaned.

But by the time Drew had returned from her stint on *Batman,* Nancy was ready for a promotion, and told Drew as much. Instead of playing housekeeper, she moved into development, reading scripts, making notes, and creating efficient filing systems. Soon enough, Nancy completely won Drew and her partner Kim over. The new recruit's motivation and zest were infectious, and within a matter of months, Drew was ready to take Nancy on the road, literally. "We drove cross-country in a Winnebago," Nancy recalled. "We left from L.A., drove for about three weeks and ended up in New Hampshire."

The young women brought a Dictaphone on their trip, and spent much of the three weeks tossing around fun concepts for future movies. "I don't know if the tapes produced any real ideas," Nancy later admitted, "but they made us feel like we could do it, we can make this happen."

Of course, learning the producer's trade would take

more than one road trip. The women of Flower Films really put their minds to the task of moviemaking. Each was prepared to study the creative, financial, and interpersonal sides of the business for as long as it took to get a real production deal in the works. Some of these cram-sessions yielded hilarious results. "We spent two years learning to speak the language and really educating ourselves," Nancy revealed. "Our first director's list, bless us, had people on it who weren't around, like Hal Ashby, whom we didn't know had died."

For the most part, however, the business partners were serious about learning all they could and collecting as many solid proposals as possible. One day, they'd have the confidence to go before a studio and ask for a production deal, and when that day came, the young women wanted to be good and ready.

In the last quarter of 1994, Drew's acting career entered a rather fallow period. Perhaps it was this lack of productive occupation that led Drew to pull the three stunts that she would never be able to live down—or, for that matter, would she particularly want to. The first shock that the nineteen-year-old siren gave the world was her face and completely nude figure on the cover of the January 1995 *Playboy*.

Upon seeing the issue, Steven Spielberg must have shaken his head and looked over at the office wall that featured the painting that a six-year-old Drew had given her newfound godfather. To express his feelings on the issue, Spielberg had his graphics people "airbrush" clothes onto the nude *Playboy* photos. This retouched magazine was then dispatched to Drew, with the dictum: "Cover up." For her part, Drew was as pleased as punch with Spielberg's reaction. "I love that," she said, "because it's funny and it's fatherly and it says something, but it doesn't make me feel bad."

While many people would disapprove of Drew's decision to bare it all, the actress had her own reasons for going through with the photo shoot. "I'm so comfortable in my skin," she said. "If you ever are lucky enough to get to that place in your life . . . you have to take advantage of it. It's not about exhibitionism. That's where it goes wrong, when it becomes wanting to show yourself, instead of just being able to."

If these words sound like something of a mission statement, maybe it's because that's exactly what they were. Within months of revealing herself in *Playboy,* Drew was once again up to her old tricks, stripping down at New York's upscale Blue Angel nightclub. Drew was out with a friend when she decided to give the club's paying customers the show of a lifetime, jumping onto the stage and performing a professional-quality striptease to a round of hoots, hollers, and thunderous applause. Of course, Drew's momentary lapse of modesty was in all the papers the very next day. "I believe in being honest with the press," she explained. "When you read in the *New York Post* that a friend and I went to our favorite strip club and did an act together, that's true. I did that, and I had so much fun doing it, and I don't regret it for a second."

Again, and just as Drew expected, there were people who frowned on her freewheeling antics. As a role model for teens, Drew was a complete washout. At twenty years of age, however, setting a proper example was the last of Drew's priorities. But contrary to what many pundits claimed, Drew's striptease was not so much an attempt to undermine her career as an expression of her freedom and joy.

Maybe it was Eric Erlandson's rock 'n' roll influence, but doing exactly as she pleased came quite naturally to Drew in the spring of '95. Just days after the Blue Angel extravaganza, Drew was invited to come on *Late Night with David Letterman*. The news sent her into a fit of giggles and frenzied nerves. Having nursed a burning crush for the sarcastic talk show host since childhood, she couldn't wait to see him. "I think that the most attractive combination a human being can contain is intellect and humor," Drew elaborated. "And he's got that. And that's what I find attractive in people. You know, I was just drawn to him."

Drew's enthusiasm for the host was apparent the night she graced the *Late Night* stage. She knew that Letterman was bound to ask her about her topless dance at the Blue Angel; what she didn't know was how she was going to respond. As it turned out, the response she ended up giving shocked even her. While describing her striptease act, Drew suddenly stopped and asked, "Would you like me to do a dance for you?"

No fool he, Letterman did not try to stop Drew from climbing up onto his desk, giving him the full frontal flash treatment and then topping it all off with a kiss on the cheek. The audience responded with boisterous cheering, while an uncharacteristically dumbstruck David Letterman could only say, "I can't thank you enough for that." His reserved words, however, belied a genuine appreciation for Drew's chutzpah. "I guess an argument can be made that it was in bad taste," Letterman quipped in a later interview, "but I have to say from a professional standpoint and also from a personal standpoint, it was certainly one of the delights of my adult life."

In Drew's opinion, the experience was one for the books—and not just because she now had a fan-for-life in David Letterman. "It was definitely the most exhilarating minute of my life," she said. "Any woman who tells me she sat next to Dave's desk and didn't want to get up and dance for him, they're lying—or just really different than me, and I can't understand them."

Had the actress thought over all the possible ramifications before leaping onto Dave's desk, chances are she would not have done it. But Drew wasn't nearly as calculating as all that. As anyone who caught that night's show could well see she was only being herself—and that was pretty cool. "I was as freaked out as [Letterman] was," Drew revealed. "I was like 'I don't know where I'm going with this one, my career could be over, oh well . . . This is worth it. I'm having too much fun.'"

Naturally, Drew's stint on the show made it into all the papers. The nationally televised display, along with her *Playboy* spread and Blue Angel striptease, would follow Drew for the rest of the millennium, if not the rest of her life. Not surprisingly, the brash young actress would harbor no regrets, saying "When I'm forty, I'm going to get the biggest kick out of looking at that."

In retrospect, it makes sense to look at Drew's wild streak(ing) as a celebration of sorts, a kind of extended twentieth birthday party. When she marked the momentous occasion on February 22, 1995, Drew reflected on how drastically her life had changed in recent years, and how many things she had to be grateful for, such as her friends, her love for Eric, her career, and her happiness. Looking around at the fifteen people who'd gathered for her birthday dinner, Drew thought to herself: "I can't believe that I'm so lucky to be surrounded by these people right now. I'm twenty years old today. I've carried myself through the years. I've made mistakes along the way, but they were the kind of mistakes that we all have to make in order to learn."

Drew had indeed come a long way. And if her uninhibited period only accomplished one thing, it made everyone forget about the drug-addled thirteen-year-old of yesterday. For the older, rehabilitated Drew, it wasn't a moment too soon.

EIGHT

Girl-Next-Door

Just as Drew was shocking the world with the full force of her fabulousness, her labors of the past year were beginning to bear fruit. The good reviews for *Boys on the Side* had been casting a glow about her acting prowess since February, and now that *Mad Love*'s May '95 release was upon her, Drew found that she was again in for more of the same. According to *Entertainment Weekly*, Drew's "good and modulated" performance in the movie even bested her showing in *Boys on the Side*. Meanwhile, *L.A. Times* critic Kevin Thomas thought that Drew was the highlight of the movie, radiating "a timeless, indelible star quality."

Meanwhile, Drew's personal life was also cresting. Her relationship with Eric Erlandson had grown very serious, very fast. In fact, in May of 1995 the two were already living together at Drew's Los Angeles home. The couple had undertaken the task of rehabilitating the ten-room house that Drew had rented out for the past seven years, going so far as to put a koi pond on the lawn. So smitten was she, that Drew actually told one interviewer that she'd "marry Eric in a heartbeat."

"It's really disgusting," Drew said. "I'm still in the throes of discovering my love. It's remarkable, I wake up every morning more in love than the day before."

Just as Drew had been attracted by Jamie Walters's stable family background, she was now irresistibly drawn to Eric's loving family. "I never thought I'd have a traditional family until I had one of my own—I know what all the fuss is about now," Drew said. "Everything else dissolves around you, and you're lost in a really safe world."

Inspired by this idyllic image of family life, Drew finally decided to reach out to her mother. Although the two hadn't had any contact for two years, Jaid had kept busy by writing *Secrets of World Class Lovers,* which she dedicated to Drew, and posing nude for *Playboy* just months after Drew's issue hit the newsstands. Although Drew has never commented on her mother's midlife crisis shenanigans, her attempts to rekindle the mother-daughter relationship would indicate that she didn't altogether disapprove. In fact, according to Jaid, Drew was actually pleased with her recent flurry of activity. "It's the best thing," Jaid effused. "She has pride in me for having written this book that she never had before. There's an ease and sweetness we never had."

Determined to make the friendship work, Drew started the healing process by writing Jaid letters. Eventually, she hoped to completely bridge the gulf that divided her from her mom. To do that, however, the Barrymores would have to start slowly. For her part, Jaid was just happy to see that her daughter was coming around. "It's pretty thrilling anytime I get a piece of correspondence from Drew," she said. "I just start crying. I'm like Niagara Falls."

Of course, relationships weren't the only thing on Drew's mind in the summer of '95. Always mindful of her career, the actress had a future to think about and recently-released movies to promote. Her publicist was inundated with calls from magazines such as *Movieline*, *Premiere*, *GQ*, and *Details*, all vying for the honor of featuring Drew on their covers. Best of all, career opportunities were popping up at every turn, and Drew could see that she'd not have to worry where her next meal, nay her next Beverly Hills estate, was coming from.

Reporters with attention-grabbing headlines on the brain did not hesitate to call 1995 "The Year of the Drew." Seeing as she had starred in three high-profile pictures within the span of six months, the appellation made perfect sense—as did the pressure that Drew felt as a result of all her success.

What to do for an encore? That was the million dollar question.

Fortunately, Drew did not have to deliberate for long. Instead of pinning her reputation on one movie, she was once again in a position to align herself with several worthwhile projects. The first of these was Woody Allen's musical revival, *Everyone Says I Love You*. Thanks to Allen's cagey tactics, however, vocally-challenged Drew had no idea that the movie would be a musical when she was breaking her back to land the role of central character Skylar. "For years, I wanted to do a musical for people who couldn't sing . . . ," Allen said to explain why he wanted to keep the musical aspect of his movie on the "down low." "I wanted it to be natural. The cab driver, the hospital patient, whoever, just the best you could do."

Blissfully unaware of the director's intentions, Drew jumped at the chance to audition for the film. She'd been a fan of Allen's for as long as she could remember and, having seen every last one of his numerous films, listed *Annie Hall, Manhattan,* and *The Purple Rose of Cairo* as some of her all-time favorites. "I am an absolute Woody Allen afficionado," she raved. "I have seen every single one of his movies at least twenty times. I can quote them all. This man has the best emotional provocation of any director in the world. He allows us to relate to people of love and relationships and human circumstance. He's so smart. . . ."

Taking part in a Woody Allen picture was a no-brainer for Drew. The director, however, was unconvinced of Drew's suitability for the role. The problem was that the name Drew Barrymore had become synonymous with dangerous and unstable characters who in no way resembled the refined, Upper East Side debutante that was Skylar. "I auditioned many times and it was really hard for Woody to see me as a debutante," Drew recalled, "and I could completely understand that, but I knew I could do this character."

Acting the part of a proper lady might have seemed a stretch for the actress whose last three appearances involved various degrees of indecent exposure and who was presently sporting a cropped, burgundy hairdo, but

Drew was adamant about snagging the highly prized role. There were no lengths to which she wouldn't go to get her way, and even her overpowering awe of the great director was not going to stop her from giving it her best shot. "I was *so* nervous," she revealed. "I was just so excited that [Woody Allen] called me in the first place, that he had an open enough mind to ask me to audition. I didn't know he knew I was even *alive*. My God, he's my hero."

Allen was ultimately won over by Drew's talent, saying that she "has the kind of gift that can't be taught. She's just naturally interesting, believable and sexy and is capable of a wide range of performances." Drew herself said she had to jump through a lot of hoops to get the role. One of those jumps led her to yet another movie, one in which she'd had neither the intention nor the desire to take part. Since *Everyone Says I Love You* was to be released by Miramax, Drew was told by Miramax chairman Harvey Weinstein that her chances of getting the role of Skylar would be considerably higher if she played team ball—namely, if she lent her name and acting chops to the Miramax-financed "indie" film *Wishful Thinking*.

The low-budget, Gen-X romantic comedy featured the dramatic talents of Jennifer Beals and Jon Stewart, but everyone knew that *Wishful Thinking* really needed someone like Drew to give it an edge in a market already wearied by *Singles* knockoffs. When filming began in the fall of '95, Drew had mixed feelings. Although she believed that she'd been railroaded into doing the movie and couldn't wait for it to wrap, her horizon was considerably brightened by the prospect of working on her first Woody Allen film.

All told, Drew had done right to compromise. But that didn't make her time on the set of *Wishful Thinking* go by any faster. In fact, she spent the entire two-month shoot feeling as if she'd been played like a Steinway grand, and deeply resenting the pressure tactics of Miramax. As soon as she had her chance, she spoke out against the injustice of it all to *Harper's Bazaar*, saying: "I was really unhappy on that movie, because I got manipulated into doing it . . . Gwyneth Paltrow had the same deal with Miramax and had to make *The Pallbearer* to get *Emma*. And it's so funny, because she totally busted Harvey Weinstein [cochairman of Miramax] in an interview. So I'm like, not only hats off to Gwyneth Paltrow but I'm going to do it, too! I got fucking manipulated into doing a goddamn movie I hated!"

Drew's grandstanding, however, came long after she'd already milked her Miramax-muse role for all its worth. Indeed, consenting to star in *Wishful Thinking* had put her in such good stead with the powerhouse production company that she was not only tapped for *Everyone Says I Love You*, but for *Scream* as well.

While Wes Craven's *Scream* trilogy may be a household name now, nary a soul outside of central casting knew anything about the movie back in 1995. Even fewer in number were those who knew how successful the franchise would become. But Drew needed only to read the script to get some inkling of the film's box office potential.

Still, crazy as she was about horror films, the savvy business woman wasn't about to let her whole future ride on what many called a "dead" genre. She knew that she wanted to be in the movie, but hesitated as to what should be the extent of her commitment. Miramax wanted her to play the heroine, Sydney Prescott. Drew, however, didn't want to shoulder the responsibility for what might very well have turned out to be a dismal flop. Instead, she suggested that she take the role of Casey Becker, the film's first victim, claiming that "I ended up choosing the smaller role, Casey Becker, just because that was really my favorite part of the movie."

The suggestion had "crazy" written all over it. After all, how can you kill off the biggest star in the movie, let alone do it in the very first scene? Then again, it was just crazy enough to work. Upon further analysis, it was decided that Drew's idea was much more than sound, it just might be the key to the whole film. "There's certain things in scary movies. You always know you're safe with someone. And I hate that," Drew explained to *People Online.* "You know? It's like—you're with Jamie Lee Curtis—you're safe! You're going to make it to Hollywood in three and you know it. I wanted to rip the carpet out from people by knowing that if I died, anyone could die, too."

Sure enough, the scene that started it all, Drew's five minutes of film, would go down as one of the most horrifying sequences in slasher movie history and catapult

Scream into the lofty position of highest-grossing horror film of all time. Best of all, it would finally prove that Drew had what it took to get the public out of their homes and into the theaters. Of course, this favorable outcome was still a ways off. Drew had to finish filming *Everyone Says I Love You* before she could so much as start thinking about the substance of her high-voltage performance for *Scream*.

After the casting for the Woody Allen movie had been completed, Drew was thrilled to learn that Goldie Hawn would be playing her mother, Alan Alda her father, and Edward Norton and Tim Roth her two love interests. While Julia Roberts would also be starring, Drew would not be in any scenes with America's ever-smiling sweetheart. But that mattered very little considering her great respect for her two leading men. "Tim is one of the finest actors," Drew said. "Talk about someone who has the ability to show their range. I have a love triangle with Tim and Edward in the film. Ha! I'm *the* luckiest girl in the world! How could you not be in love with those two men? Woody lets you improvise, and those two guys are extraordinary at it."

Her time on the set only intensified Drew's feelings for her costars. Roth and Norton had all the qualities that Drew admired. The guys were much more than just great actors, they were great friends. "Between Tim Roth and Ed Norton, I wouldn't know who to choose," Drew effused, "they're both so amazing. Those guys are both deep and so funny. The way to my heart is to make me laugh. I've worked with assholes before and it's no fun, but I won't name any names. Usually the most talented and extraordinary people also tend to be the most generous."

Clearly, Drew wasn't shy when it came to singing the guys' praises. When it came to singing her verses, however, her attitude was far less accommodating. In fact, Drew admitted that when she first heard the movie was a musical, her initial instinct had been "to puke on the floor."

The fact was that Drew simply wasn't partial to musicals. Never had been. "I have to be honest," she said. "I wasn't a big fan of musicals before this, but I thought, 'The one person who could pull this off is Woody Allen.' The thing he does in this movie that I love the most is he allows you to laugh when people break into song and dance. I think that's important, because I want to laugh at people who start doing that."

For all the good-natured fun that a musical had to offer, Drew was still convinced that her vocal stylings should not, under any circumstances, be inflicted upon a paying public. Since years of heavy smoking had left her with a voice that in no way matched that of her character, Drew decided that she couldn't possibly sing her own songs and petitioned Woody Allen for clemency. "I've got a really deep, raspy voice, and my character's voice was pretty and pure, so I couldn't sing like that," she explained. "I wanted to change my voice for her, because she is so sweet and pure. It was hard, because I didn't want people to think I didn't take my job seriously."

In the end, Drew prevailed and hers was the only

singing voice to never grace the *Everyone Says I Love You* soundtrack. Fortunately, her fears of being thought irresponsible proved unfounded. Everyone on the set, from the director to the actors to the craft-service people, fell head over heels in love with the winsome young actress. Edward Norton, for one, was positively floored by Drew's good vibrations. "Drew has a more sincere instinct for giving than anyone of our generation I've met in this business," he attested. "She has forged this terrific positivity toward life, and a spiritual density and grace, out of nothing."

The reviews that would accompany the film's December '96 release date would echo Norton's sentiments, praising Drew's performance as one of the picture's most delightful surprises.

December 1996 would be a banner month for Drew Barrymore. Besides *Everyone Says I Love You,* Wes Craven's *Scream* was also being released to popular, if not always critical, acclaim. As much attention as the film received, it was Drew's over-the-top portrayal of the frantic and traumatized Casey Becker that won the most enthusiastic accolades from audiences nationwide.

The success of Drew's performance was no accident. Although it only took her seven days to shoot the scene, the actress had put a great deal of thought both into the choosing of her character and the analysis of her motivation. After thinking it through, Drew decided that the slaying of Casey Becker would be all the more terrifying if she played the role as honestly as possible, without any of the clichés that make most slasher flicks so laughable.

"I could go ultimate camp, B movie, wild luscious, candy-apple, dripping freak, you know? I could do anything. Because a lot of girls in scary movies they like slide under the stairs, kick [the killers] in the sternum, do anything, run down the stairs. Uh-uh. I would not be able to move. I'd be screaming, crying, and freaking out. I know I'd want to fight for my life but I think I'd probably die of a heart attack before the killer even got to me," Drew stated. "I wanted to play it that way. . . ." Working with Wes Craven on the intense scene "was the greatest seven days of my life."

Paradoxically enough, shooting her *Scream* sequence was both the best and the worst of times for Drew. Since she insisted on going through the real emotions of a stalking victim, the weeklong shoot was the most nerve-racking experience of her career. "I was very honest with myself," she explained. "Because I think that was the most important thing for me to do in this movie, and although I *love* slasher films, they're my favorite, and I love really scary movies, I didn't want it to be campy. I wanted it to be real. . . . You know I did this thing where I would jump up and down and get hyperventilated, and the whole crew made fun of me. I looked like a total geek."

The blond wig that Drew was made to don over her then-jet-black locks also helped to get her into Casey Becker's hapless head-cheerleader character. Even the fake blood that was poured over her clothes went a long way towards convincing Drew that she really was being pursued by a psycho killer. And if all this weren't enough, Wes Craven's artistic direction was the pièce de résistance, forcing Drew into the horrific state of mind that she'd set out to achieve at the beginning of the shoot. So, it should come as no surprise that when filming on the sequence wrapped, Drew felt as if every ounce of anger, fear, and frustration had been drained from her body. "I won't have PMS for five years because of that movie—which is great, by the way—but it was very cathartic in the end," Drew asserted. "I would have never done the job if not for Wes Craven. Wes is the most amazing director. He's really talented."

In the time that it took Drew to finish her scene, she and Craven had united in a sort of mutual admiration society. Watching Drew work, Wes Craven could tell that Drew's depiction was pure genius. Struck by her overwhelming talent and stage presence, he expressed his gratitude to the actress who'd make his movie a smash by saying that she "certainly understands a hell of a lot more than other kids her age. There is an emotionality and vulnerability. She knows what is of value and what is not. And for another thing, she's a legend in her own time."

The debut of *Scream* would only add to that legend. In the eyes of the public, Drew became far larger-than-life. Her classic performance has been said to rival that of Shelley Duvall in *The Shining*, and the marketing ploy that gave Drew top billing only to kill her off in the first scene worked like a charm. Audiences were scared witless, and kept coming back again and again, until the box office gross had climbed well above the hundred million dollar mark. More important, the film ushered in a new era of teensploitation. Horror films with sexy, young stars taken right off the TV screens became all the rage (think *I Know What You Did Last Summer, Disturbing Behavior,* and *Urban Legend*). But the slice-and-dice genre would soon be done to death, and teen heartthrobs would be recast in romantic comedies such as *She's All That* and *Ten Things I Hate About You,* whereupon Drew would once again rule the school. And considering that it was her scene in *Scream* that launched the whole teen-power movement in the first place, most would agree that her place at the head of the class was well earned.

After finishing off her *Wishful Thinking–Everyone Says I Love You–Scream* acting triathalon, Drew found that she was more in demand than ever. In fact, she didn't have a moment to spare. Her old friend Tamra Davis was helming the director's chair on *Best Men,* a low-budget bank-heist film, and with a cast that consisted mostly of TV actors such as Dean Cain and Andy Dick, as well as little-known up-and-comers such as Luke Wilson, Davis needed Drew to give the movie some of that all-important star power.

Since *Best Men* was a buddy picture featuring five male leads, Drew was relegated to a key supporting role. In light of her loyalty to Tamra, it was a role she was happy to take. And as it turned out, playing Hope, the loyal fiancée of Luke Wilson's character, gave Drew a much-needed opportunity to focus on the strong and positive aspects of her personality—just the thing after that harrowing *Scream* shoot. Better still, the movie introduced her to Luke Wilson, the guy who'd soon become her greatest love of all.

Although Drew had been involved in a long-term relationship with Eric Erlandson, their soaring careers had forced them to spend a lot of time apart. Sadly, the frequent separations proved as fatal to this romance as they had to Drew's relationship with Jamie Walters. Eric's life was on the West Coast, whereas the filming of *Wishful Thinking* and *Everyone Says I Love You* kept Drew in New York for months at a time. Indeed, the actress became so "New York" that she finally had to trade in her hotel room for a lease on an apartment in Manhattan's hip West Village.

In the end, after having spent nearly two years as a couple, Drew and Eric parted as friends in the spring of 1996. "There are relationships that end and you not only remain close, but get closer in a different way," Drew revealed.

The amicable split made things considerably easier since, during her time with Eric, Drew and Courtney Love had gone from tolerating each other's presence to forging a lifelong friendship. After Courtney named Drew as godmother to her daughter, Frances Bean Cobain, the women's friendship underwent intense scrutiny in the tabloid press. But nothing could drive a rift into what was by all accounts a deep and solid friendship. "She's part of the group that lives inside my heart," expressed Drew. "But there are still times when we talk and I'll be like, 'I can't believe you'd say that—

who are you?' or she'll say, 'Omigod, you are so full of craziness.'"

The way that Courtney described her feelings for Drew proved that the actress would be hard-pressed to find a more adoring or loyal gal pal. Although Drew's wild girl phase was on the wane and she was still as drug-free as they come, motherhood had certainly not mellowed the hard-living Courtney Love. Still, there was much common ground to be found. In fact, the friendship was a continuous source of satisfaction for both women. "She's like a sister to me," Courtney declared, "somebody I would really fight to protect. She brings that out in all sorts of people. She really has taught me to simplify my life a little more, to take pleasure out of stupid stuff that's just fun—having barbecues, having picnics, going to the movies, having sleep-overs."

Some months after breaking up with Eric, Drew found herself once again in the throes of passion on the set of *Best Men*. A certifiable love addict, it seemed as though she had a hard time going so much as a year without getting swept off her feet. An unrepentant Drew admitted as much when she stated that she was "a loveaholic now and of all the holics you can be, that's preferable."

A longtime fan of Drew's movies, not to mention her *Playboy* layout, Luke Wilson was immediately struck by the warmth that Drew radiated on the set. She was so friendly and outgoing that he felt absolutely no qualms about approaching her for a date towards the tail end of the movie shoot. "I just kinda asked her out," Luke recalled. "It just seemed natural. She makes you feel that at ease. She made so much of an effort in her dealings with people. She's so smart and funny and ready to laugh, she has a way of making you forget all the stuff you may have heard or read [about her]."

Although Drew was a top-billed star and Luke still a little-known actor, the relationship flourished. Luke had won the attention of the film community for his work on the acclaimed indie film *Bottle Rocket* and was not threatened by Drew's star power. Working alongside his brothers Owen C. and Andrew Wilson, he was steadily gaining the industry's esteem and had every reason to believe that his name would one day grace marquees all over America.

In fact, soon after wrapping *Best Men*, Luke was hired to star in another small but heartfelt film called *Home Fries*. As the film featured none other than his current flame Drew Barrymore, it certainly seemed as if destiny had struck again. "I didn't know they were an item when I cast Luke," insisted *Home Fries* director Dean Parisot.

Parisot was not alone. Since both Luke and Drew had agreed to keep a tight lid on their goings-on, no one was aware that the two were anything more than friends.

After coming off *Best Men*, Drew's relationship with Luke Wilson progressed rather slowly due to her on-screen involvement with Adam Sandler. The two were filming *The Wedding Singer* and, for the time being, the role of Julia demanded all of Drew's attention. Set in the Eighties, the romantic yet vintage-Adam-Sandler comedy had Drew playing a purehearted waitress whom Adam Sandler, as the wedding singer, saves from marrying the wrong man. The script had all the makings of a hit, and the character of Julia represented everything that Drew wanted to branch into—namely, the opposite of Miss Poison Ivy. "Right now, I don't want to do anything heavy," Drew explained. "I just want to laugh."

As a knee-jerk reaction to spending some four years playing bad girls, Drew wanted nothing more than a string of movies that featured her as the lovable girl-next-door. Thanks to Woody Allen, who'd started her on the path to redemption with the role of Skylar, Drew was finally getting exactly what she wanted: Julia was nothing less than a dream girl. "She's fun, she's light-spirited, she's not heavy," Drew said of her character. "She can find the optimism and the fun in any scenario. I love that about her . . . I find that quite refreshing. I aspire to that myself. It was an honor to play her because she taught me a lot."

In sketching out her character, Drew collaborated closely with Adam Sandler. The two had a great deal of respect for each other's diverse talents and became true buddies on and off the set. Like most of Adam Sandler's movies, *The Wedding Singer* was a wonderful work environment. Since Sandler liked to hire his old college pals to produce, direct, and write, the set was like a big, happy family and no one appreciated this atmosphere more than Drew herself. "In the morning, people were smiling when they came to work," she said. "Every day on the set, people would clap when everybody came on. And we would laugh all day long. No one at the end of

the day was like: 'Get me out of here, I have had it'—
even out of exhaustion alone. Adam kept everybody
laughing all day long, every day. It just was one of the
most incredible working experiences I have ever had."

It would also turn out to be one of the most fiscally
beneficial. After completing her work on *The Wedding
Singer,* Drew's asking price climbed to a whopping three
million dollars per picture. The drastic hike in her salary
was due in no small part to the movie's astounding success—after only a few weeks in theaters, *The Wedding
Singer* would rake in over one hundred million.

Of course, since Drew had already signed to the sixteen million-dollar-budget *Home Fries,* she'd have to
wait for her next project to cash in on the big payday.
Meanwhile, *Home Fries* offered other incentives—
specifically, the chance to star opposite and fall madly in
love with her boyfriend, Luke Wilson.

The dark comedy had Drew playing the role of Sally,
a fast-food restaurant employee who's nearly nine
months pregnant with a married man's baby. Luke Wilson plays Dorian, one of the married man's two sons,
who falls in love with Sally before finding out that she'd
had an affair with his father and is, therefore, about to
give birth to his half brother.

To play the character of Sally, Drew sought out a
rather unusual inspiration—the syrupy-sweet Dolly Parton. Following her muse all the way to Parton's
Nashville-based theme park, Dollywood, the actress
had no trouble immersing herself in the mentality of a
southern belle. The one aspect of the Austin-based
shoot that did give Drew some pause was the preg-

nancy. Required to don a forty-pound pregnancy suit, she recalled that "it was so awkward to maneuver in that suit, but at least I got to take it off every night. There wasn't a day that went by that I didn't wonder what it would be like if I couldn't unstrap that demon." Neither was the costume the only rough patch in *Home Fries'* filming. In one scene, Drew and Luke find themselves in Lamaze class, taking their characters through the motions of proper breathing technique. Since it was a pivotal sequence, the one in which Sally and Dorian are supposed to fall in love, everything had to be perfect. Imagine director Dean Parisot's chagrin when he learned that his two stars were in the midst of a lover's quarrel. "Dozens of crew members came rushing to me," he recalled, "saying everything from they were fighting to they'd broken up. It was my greatest fear come true."

But spat or no spat, the show had to go on. For the good of the film, Drew and Luke turned their frowns upside down and went to work. Instead of turning in a stunted and tension-filled performance, the actors came alive under the glare of the lights. Pretty soon their feelings of hostility were history, and the two were looking as if they'd just discovered paradise in each other's eyes. "We watched Drew and Luke fall madly in love that day," Parisot said. "The more times they did that scene, the more it was obvious to them and us that they felt something very special for each other and it's captured on film forever."

Ever since that fateful day, Drew has looked upon *Home Fries* as one of the most special projects she'd ever worked on. Her relationship with Luke would out-last every one of her past romances, and would go down as the most significant relationship of her life thus far. Some two years hence, upon the movie's fall '98 release, Drew would go on record to say that "It would be really wonderful if some day Luke and I could show our grandchildren *Home Fries* as some kind of home movie."

Perhaps her statements were premature, but that's Drew in a nutshell. Never shy when it comes to showing affection, she's worn her heart on her sleeve ever since she first fell head over Hush Puppies for Steven Spielberg at the grand old age of six.

NINE

Superstar

Drew was being hailed for her gritty performance in *Scream* and already had *Best Men, The Wedding Singer,* and *Home Fries* in the can and ready to go when she appeared at the December '96 premiere of *Everyone Says I Love You.* The past few weeks had been a public relations nightmare. Not that anything was wrong, quite the opposite. With two movies hitting theaters in the span of one month, Drew's career was going so well that she'd been doing nothing but publicity the whole time. It had been one long month of press junkets, talk show appearances, and magazine cover shoots.

Only after the premiere would Drew finally have a chance to take a long-overdue vacation. Although her affair with Luke Wilson was still very hush-hush, her many interviews revealed that she was indeed seeing someone, a young actor whose name she refused to divulge. Drew spoke about her two-year-plan to move to Texas with her new beau and start a family. "I've been seeing him for about six months," she said in one interview, "and I'm madly, madly, madly in love. I've totally met the person I want to have children with. Without question."

At the Woody Allen premiere, Drew was still thinking about her first holiday visit to the Wilson family's
homestead in Fredericksburg, Texas, when she heard
the news that would define the next year of her life: a
revised version of Cinderella was going to be made into
a movie, and the title role had yet to be cast. "I'll never
forget hearing about the project," Drew reminisced. "I
was at the Woody Allen premiere [of *Everyone Says I
Love You*], and after that I was going nuts for a month
hoping that I would get an offer. It's every girl's fantasy
to do this part."

Worrying about landing the role and about making a
good impression on the Wilsons, Drew was a ball of
nerves when she finally got to Luke's family home that
Christmas. Luke's mom, dad, two brothers, and grandma
were all home for the holidays. Looking around at this
happy, fun-loving clan made Drew yearn for their acceptance as well as for a family of her own. (While she and
her dad had reestablished some contact, Drew's attempt
to correspond with her mom had failed and the two were
again at odds.) Comparing her own upbringing with that
of Luke put Drew in an uncharacteristically quiet and re-
flective mood that did not go unnoticed by her attentive
boyfriend. "The first Christmas, she was a little nervous," recalled Luke. "I remember thinking, how could
this, of all things, make you nervous? Then I realized,
maybe she wasn't used to this. Maybe it made her think
about her own family. And she loved it, but it also made
her a little bit sad."

After spending Christmas with the Wilsons, Drew

was completely hooked on their lifestyle. In fact, no sooner had she returned to the wheelings and dealings of Hollywood than she was already thinking about getting back to the Texas ranch. "I think I'll be living in Texas soon," she mused. "Fredericksburg, Texas: It's this beautiful little town. . . . I like being so close to nature there."

Much as Drew despised the phoniness of showbiz, she could never deny that making movies was her calling and one true passion. Her overriding zest for the role of Cinderella served as a reality check. Sure, she could be one of those actors whose primary residence is somewhere in Montana or Utah, but she loved her job too much to ever turn her back on the industry. "Hollywood is so shallow and mean, and I have as little to do with it as possible," she asserted. "So many actors are just in it for the money and the glitz and the stardom—I just don't get it. I'm not in it for that. I'm in it to be a good employee. It's a job that lets me be creative and fulfilled and it also allows me to do important things as far as the world is concerned . . . making a difference with people and being a philanthropist, being an advocate of good causes."

True to her words, Drew spent countless hours volunteering on behalf of the causes nearest and dearest to her heart. In fact, she was as passionate about her activism as she was about her boyfriend, her latest film role, or Flessy and Templeton, the two puppies that she'd rescued while staying in New York. "I was at a flea market, and this guy had a box of puppies he was trying to give away," Drew recounted. "They mean just everything to me."

Drew had had a soft spot for animals for as long as she could remember. Now that she was an adult, Drew decided to do her part by contributing her time and money to the Wildlife Waystation, a wild animal rescue organization. As a strict vegan, she also refused to eat any meat and wouldn't even dream of wearing leather, suede, or fur. Whenever a reporter queried Drew about her vegan ways, she jumped at the chance to speak out in defense of animals. "I don't eat meat, fish, or dairy. . . I do this because I love animals and I don't want to eat them or wear them. I made this choice, and I don't miss anything at all about it. . . . It's just my own personal crusade, you know, and if someone doesn't understand, then I can try to explain it to them, but only the belief and education is going to make you do something."

Of course, animals weren't the only beneficiaries of Drew's goodwill. As a teen fan favorite, Drew had the power to change young lives for the better. It was a responsibility she took to heart. When the Female Health Foundation approached Drew to be the spokesperson for female condoms, she didn't hesitate. Although the job would take some doing, calling as it did for Drew to appear in commercials promoting female condoms and even to address college students about safe sex and sexually transmitted diseases, she was certain that she'd found a cause worth celebrating. "I'm thrilled to be part of an educational group, the Female Health Foundation," Drew said. "It funds clinics all over the world because it's associated with the United Nations, and it's distributing hundreds of thousands of female condoms to women all over the world. I always think how truly lucky I am because an opportunity like this does not come about very often, so I do as much with it as I can."

Where Drew found the time is anyone's guess. Devoted girlfriend, ambitious actress, and tireless activist, Drew managed to squeeze yet another major title into her already extensive repertoire. Plus she was fast on her way to earning her first producer's credit!

Although Kim Greitzer, Drew's first partner in Flower Films, had decamped in 1996, Drew and Nancy Juvonen had grown closer than ever and fell into an easy working groove. The two young women were never out of touch for long. Even when Drew was on vacation, she made certain to check in with Nancy and see if anything of interest was coming down the pipeline. For Drew, reconciling her unease with Hollywood with her love for filmmaking was easy. "I don't show up at every public function," she explained, "but I love the business side of [the entertainment industry]. Like, if you read it in the trades, you should have known it a month before. It's why I formed my company, because I understand it can go away and you need to build your own foundation."

For the most part, laying her own groundwork meant seeking out her own film projects. Drew had a few ideas that she was toying with, such as *Like a Lady* which she described as "Pygmalion meets the Wizard of Oz" and *Born to Shop*, a story about shopping for the perfect parents. Her hands-down favorite, however, was *All She Wanted,* the true tale of Brandon Teena, a young woman who decides to go through life posing as a man only to wind up brutally raped and murdered as a result. Drew was so determined to get the rights to this story that she hardly noticed how many other people had been struck by the same headlines. Instead of keeping her business confidential, Drew unwittingly ensured that she'd learn the "loose lips sink ships" lesson the hard way by telling anyone within earshot about her plans to portray Brandon Teena. As early as December '96, Drew was already discussing the would-be film in interviews and saying that "Playing a boy would be the biggest challenge of my life."

Of course, as most people are by now no doubt aware, this was one project that Drew was not destined to win. The same, however, could not be said for the coveted role of Cinderella. After spending a month with her stomach tied up in too many knots for even Houdini to escape, Drew's fears were finally laid to rest when she received a three million dollar offer to play Danielle de Barberac, the heroine of *Ever After: A Cinderella Story.* Although Drew had been anxious about losing out on this role of a lifetime, it had actually been her interest in the movie that convinced Twentieth Century Fox executives to go ahead with the picture. "It didn't seem new or interesting until Drew came along," attested studio chairman Bill Mechanic. "She's edgy, and she's not a victim."

Indeed, Drew was probably the most famous female survivor to walk the earth since Cinderella herself. By her twenty-second birthday, the whole of the United States stood in awe of Drew's inspiring comeback. Of course, when the film world got wind of Drew's involvement in *Ever After,* the project was suddenly surrounded by the kind of buzz that no amount of money can buy. With Drew in the title role, anyone could foresee that *Ever After* was going to take the box office by storm.

Drew's Danielle de Barbarac was not going to be your average, run-of-the-mill airy-fairy Cinderella. The young actress was intent on bringing an extra dimension to the character. This was going to be a smart and feisty Cinderella, the kind of woman who needs no fairy godmother to get her Prince Charming. "I didn't want to portray a girl who sort of sat around and wished for what she wanted, and it magically came to her," Drew explained. "In this version, it's really her brains and the fact that she's well read that make her win in the end. It has nothing to do with anything that could be aesthetic or, to be honest, shallow . . . There are so many pressures that are put upon young women. Whatever we can do to alleviate that and [help women] feel beautiful about who [they] are inside, which is the only beauty there truly is, is so nice."

Ever After would be shot in the glorious countryside of the south of France, and Drew counted the months until the shoot's September start date. Although the part seemed to have fallen right into her lap, Drew had had to pay a steep price to play Cinderella. Originally, she was supposed to spend the fall of 1997 on the set of what would become Woody Allen's *Celebrity*. Hers would have been the role of the free-spirited and capricious heartbreaker that eventually went to Winona Ryder. Drew had been one of the first actors that Allen had cast in the picture. Now, she had to sacrifice, and it was by no means easy. According to her spokesperson, the "decision was very difficult for Drew. She had a tremendous experience working for Mr. Allen last time and hopes to work with him again in the very near future."

Despite her initial reservations, Drew clearly wasn't about to second-guess what everyone agreed had been the right decision. But if Drew was confident before, she became even more convinced when she learned that Oscar-winner Anjelica Huston had signed on to play her wicked stepmother. For Drew, one of the most exciting aspects of the collaboration was that as the daughter of the venerable director John Huston, Anjelica Huston was also the progeny of Hollywood royalty. "I got so into the idea of Huston and Barrymore working together—our ancestors looking down on us," she enthused. "I was like, 'Let's go!'"

As usual, Drew's enthusiasm was contagious. Within the first few weeks of filming, everyone on the set of *Ever After* was smitten with the picture's winsome star. Although she'd worked with director Andy Tennant five years before, back when he directed her in *The Amy Fisher Story,* Drew had to win over the rest of the cast and crew from scratch. To inject the production with a much-needed dose of good cheer, Drew went out of her way to provide extra snacks for all involved and even threw a Halloween party. "Everyone was sort of segregated in their groups, but I did my best to bring people together," she said. "When you're making a movie, you're actually with these people for three months, every day, day in, day out, all day long. I think this is a functioning, working family, and that is so great."

Among the people blown away by Drew's unpretentious attitude was Dougray Scott, her onscreen love interest. "She's not the Hollywood starlet she could be," Scott said. "She is one of the most generous people I've ever met." Despite their onscreen enmity, Anjelica Huston was also a great fan, saying that Drew "has a wonderful relationship with the camera, not so much as a chameleon, but like Jack Nicholson, she has that star quality."

At one point, Huston was so swept up in Drew's moving performance that she even broke into tears. The tear-jerking scene was the one in which Danielle confronts her stepmother about whether she'd ever loved her. For Drew, investing the dialogue with authenticity was all too easy; the face-off exactly mirrored her feelings toward her own parents and the way in which she'd been raised. "In *Ever After,* when I'm dealing with pain with my stepmother . . . ," recalled Drew, "I totally think of my own life and how much I am in need to have that conversation with my own mother."

Certainly, Drew's family life was in a perpetual state of flux. Sometimes she'd be doing her best to mend her relationship with Jaid, other times she'd refuse to speak to her mother altogether. While her relationship with her father, in which Drew saw herself as his parent, was somewhat more stable, it hardly made her feel safe and secure. John Barrymore used to call his daughter once or twice a year to see how she was doing and, more important, to ask for financial assistance. Recently, however, he'd come out of seclusion and moved into a space above his daughter's garage. "I called him and asked, 'If I got myself a little house, would you consider living there?'" Drew revealed. "He sort of moaned delightfully—which led me to believe it would be okay. It's weird because we've never lived together."

But judging by Drew's statements of just a few months later, the extreme proximity would do little to bring the two closer together. "I'm closer to my parents now, but no one in my family is really going to be there for one another. It's too late. I thought about whether I wanted to be a really resentful person, but it's just poison, and you just have to let it go. I love them, and I hope they're proud of me, but none of us can really tolerate one another. But that's cool. A lot of families are like that."

To get on with her life, Drew had to create surrogate families for herself. She found these satisfying substitutes on every one of her film sets, at her production company and, of course, in Fredericksburg, Texas. For Drew and Luke, escaping the rat race of Hollywood for the wide open spaces of Texas became a favorite tradition. The two would abscond to the small town for every family holiday, and the holiday season of '97 was no different. Having spent the duration of the *Ever After* shoot away from her love, Drew was doubly excited to see him that Thanksgiving. "I don't eat meat, but I know they do—and that'll be great," Drew said of the

Wilsons' Thanksgiving feast. "I'll eat stuffing! I love stuffing!"

No longer trying to keep her love for Luke a secret, Drew spoke openly about their relationship and about her strong feelings. The couple was seen laughing together at premieres and parties. And with Luke's name always on the tip of Drew's tongue, theirs was as happy a relationship as Drew had ever been able to forge. All things considered, when time came to ring in 1998, Drew was at the top of her game. "I feel great," she said. "I feel so unscrewed up."

TEN

Power Player

As the new year dawned, Drew had many reasons to celebrate, not the least of which was her newfound status within the Hollywood hierarchy. In September '97, Drew had finally gotten her fondest wish: to be a producer. With a development deal at Twentieth Century Fox's Fox 2000 division, Flower Films was now officially in full bloom.

Although *Born to Shop*, the first project that Drew pitched to Fox 2000, would never get the green light treatment, it wasn't the script but Drew herself who caught the studio's attention. Carla Hacken, a senior vice president at Fox 2000, had been impressed with the would-be producer ever since their first meeting. They were having a business dinner to discuss Drew's projects, but were perpetually interrupted by adoring fans who just had to get a word in edgewise. "Drew was so nice to every person, so unruffled," Hacken recounted. "And each time, she was able to go directly back to our conversation: 'As I was saying, my take on the script . . .' She handled it with such grace and poise. She was so *adult*."

Having won the studio's backing, Drew and business partner Nancy Juvonen were ready for action. Since Drew was in the south of France filming *Ever After*, however, the task of hiring and setting up shop had fallen to Nancy. By the time Drew returned from her European jaunt, the company had already grown to a staff of five, and the scripts were pouring in at the rate of twenty per week. One of these screenplays bore the title *Never Been Kissed;* for Nancy it was love at first read. So enamored was she that she couldn't wait for office hours to share the good news. "I pitched her the story one night when all of *The Wedding Singer* guys were over at my house," Nancy attested. "I was too excited to wait."

That night, Drew settled in and got to reading. As she flipped the pages of the script, she found herself identifying with the main character and hoping for a happy ending. For anyone who has not seen the movie, the plot revolves around Josie Geller, a young *Chicago Sun-Times* copy editor who dreams of becoming a reporter. The unthinkable happens when Josie's boss sends her to a local high school on an undercover assignment to find out what the "cool" kids are doing. Only problem is that Josie had been distinctly "uncool" in high school, so much so that she'd even been saddled with the nickname of Josie Grossie. The screenplay's lighthearted treatment of Josie's plight to win over the popular crowd and the lessons she learns along the way recalled Drew's own bitter experiences as a schoolgirl, and spoke to her in a way that few other scripts had. "I feel like I'm so in touch with what it's like to feel awkward. I can understand that feeling," Drew explained. "I related to the script so much. I wanted to talk about, for one, feeling good about who you are and naturally embracing that. A person's looks are never going to make you love them or like them."

As soon as she'd finished reading, Drew was determined to bring this script to the big screen. The screenplay had put her in such a good mood that she was still walking on air the next day. When she breezed into the Sunset Boulevard offices of Flower Films, Drew only had one thing on her mind.

"I read it," she told an expectant Nancy. "I love it. Let's do it!"

Easier said than done. Although Drew and Nancy were the undisputed heads of Flower Films, their deal with Fox 2000 required that the studio execs sanction their film projects. In other words, the Fox people had to be on board if *Never Been Kissed* was ever to leave the station.

Taking it upon herself to convince the brass of the script's sundry commercial merits, Drew was dismayed to learn that while Fox liked the screenplay, their ideas for the role of Josie did not jibe with her own. The studio wanted to cast an actress that would be more believable as a nerd than the beloved Drew Barrymore, but Drew had the courage of her conviction—she stood her ground and convinced studio execs that she was the very person for the role. "Drew kept talking about a caterpillar who turns into a butterfly," recalled Fox executive vice president Kevin McCormick, "which is a story she connects to."

As Drew saw it, the story wasn't about an unattractive girl getting a miracle makeover, but about a highly sensitive late bloomer who finally comes into her own. Neither did the first-time producer see *Never Been Kissed* as a "teen movie." In her mind's eye, the script was about self-discovery. "Who are you on the inside?" Drew explained. "That's where everything lies. All the beauty, all the ugliness, and the outside is just the shell that you work with. And I loved [the idea of] a movie that explored that. Because whether it's societal or because of pressures from other people, I thought that high school was the perfect venue for that self-exploration, self-examination, and how to learn to love yourself."

In all actuality, playing Josie, the much-abused nerd, was but a stone's throw away from playing Danielle, the put-upon Cinderella, in *Ever After*. Both movies addressed the subject of inner beauty and concluded with the triumph of character over adversity. Odd as it seemed, there was no denying that Drew was now bent on becoming a proper role model for young women.

In March, Drew's big date movie, *The Wedding Singer,* was still packing them in at the theaters when she showed up at the 1998 Academy Awards looking like the very picture of her onscreen, "dream girl" character Julia. As *The Wedding Singer* was climbing unimpeded to its eventual 100 million dollars plus box office gross, Drew appeared to be doing all she could to live up to the wholesome reputation that she'd secured via this surprise blockbuster. Wearing daisies in her blond pixie hairdo, a $250 off-the-rack dress on her butterfly-tattooed back and some dirt in her shoes to stay "connected to the earth," Drew didn't need to be nominated for an actual Oscar to wind up as one of the most photographed women of the evening.

From that point on, Drew went from appearing on the covers of men's lifestyle magazines to being the chosen It girl of such teen-friendly fare as *Sugar, Seventeen, Mademoiselle,* and *Teen.* Finally, even *Time* magazine had to concede that, after all, "she's not a bad role model." The image transformation was as drastic as Hollywood had seen since, well, since Drew's friend Courtney Love decided to doff her grungie baby-doll dresses and go glam. Except in Drew's case, there didn't seem to be anything calculated or unnatural about the metamorphosis. In fact, the reinvention seemed to be a simple case of life imitating art—like so many of her characters, twenty-three-year-old Drew had found herself at last.

With the shooting of *Never Been Kissed* scheduled to begin that summer, Drew had her preproduction work cut out for her. As the first movie to come out of Flower Films, *Never Been Kissed* had to be a success, or it was curtains for Drew's producing career. With all her responsibilities, how Drew ever managed to devote herself so completely to the movie's production is anyone's guess, but by all accounts that's exactly what she did. "I was involved in every aspect of making the film: cast, production design, costumes," she said. "My brain felt like a speeding train."

No doubt, casting had to be one of the film's most demanding jobs. Although Drew already had the lead, there was a whole cast of characters that needed to be filled. Auditioning actors, dealing with schedule conflicts, and convincing the studio to support any and all casting decisions was a mammoth job, but Drew wasn't above handling it herself. According to Michael Vartan, the actor who portrayed Drew's love interest in *Never Been Kissed,* it was Drew who went to bat for him and got him the role. "She's one of the main reasons that I got this part," he said. "I heard through the grapevine that she really fought to get me in this film. To a studio, I'm still a nobody, so this is a great opportunity. It's funny how, when nice people are at the head of something, it sort of trickles down."

Michael Vartan, however, wasn't the only cast member to fall for Drew's many charms. LeeLee Sobieski, who was brought on to play the "queen of the nerds," said, "There's no other actress I look up to as much as Drew. I'm so amazed by her, because she's had a hard life and she's still become the sweetest person in the world. If you give her a compliment, she makes you feel like you've told her the most special thing in her entire life. Then she'll come right back and give you ten compliments."

Much of the praise heaped upon Drew's shoulders was due to her laid-back producing style. While she rarely hesitated to fight for what she believed in, Drew was not the type to flex her muscle just for the fun of it. Working alongside director Raja Gosnell, as well as her partners and her casting director, Drew didn't have any problem sublimating her own ego for the good of the project. "It's very empowering to have the opportunity to make so many decisions, but it's still a democracy," she maintained. "And majority rules. You choose your battles and stick to certain things that you're passionate about. Being a problem solver is so wonderful, it's a wonderful opportunity for that. It's a great thing to be able to create an atmosphere where actors are free to do what they want, and improvise a little."

Certainly, with Drew, everyone always felt free to go their own way. Take for instance, David Arquette's request that people not cheer after every single one of his takes, a tradition that Drew had implemented to make the long hours of filming more fun. When David, who played Drew's cool older brother in the movie, balked at the idea, saying, "Oh, my God! This can't go on! We can't cheer every time we do a damn take. If we do, I'm gonna walk out of here thinking I'm Lord Olivier or something." Drew and the rest of the cast were only too happy to oblige him. While everyone else got cheers after the director yelled "cut," David was told that he "sucked."

As busy as Drew was during the summer shoot, she still found time to play Pocket Yahtzee with her cast and crew mates, and to promote the July '98 release of *Ever After*. Since *Ever After* was the first big-budget film that Drew had ever headlined on her own, there was simply no getting out of her publicity duties. She had to prove that she was worth her three million dollars and then some, and to do that she had to get out there and spread the word. Within the first two months of the film's release, it became obvious that Drew was worth every last cent of her paycheck—*Ever After* racked up over sixty million dollars in box office receipts.

While a lesser woman might have crumbled under the sheer weight of all this responsibility, the nonstop activity only served to reenergize Drew. Putting her personal life on hold for the time being, Drew jumped headlong into her various projects, and realized that hard work was a reward all its own. "The work was so much fun. It was so great. It takes up every second of your time and you never get upset for a second. In fact, you're like, 'More, more—more hours in the day!'"

No wonder her coworkers were amazed. Here was this self-avowed dreamer, a romantic Pisces through and through, a young woman who many still considered a flake, here she was taking care of business like a bona fide movie mogul. "When I first met her, I used to say she was an eight-year-old boy and a forty-year-old woman in the same body," Nancy Juvonen recalled. "Now I see a mature young businesswoman who is not only looking after her own best interests [but] also has a lot of serious people asking that she look after their best interests, too. And she's doing it."

Of course, this workaholism was bound to strain Drew's relationship with Luke eventually. Seeing so little of each other couldn't have been easy for either of them, as Drew let slip when she said, "I do believe in love at first sight. But I also believe in, 'How do you keep it going?' How do you keep a consistent, healthy relationship going that's communicative and has compromise, yet allows you to remain the individual [he] fell in love with?"

In the summer of '98, Drew had far too little time to spend on the pondering of these questions. Every waking moment was dedicated to staying sane while both executive producing and starring in *Never Been Kissed*.

When it was all finally over, Drew felt relieved to have completed her first Flower Films production "on time and under budget," and excited to spend more time with Luke as well as her three adorable dogs. It had been nearly a year since she'd bought a spacious, solar-heated home, complete with two-and-a-half acres of land, in Los Angeles' upscale Coldwater Canyon. And here at long last was Drew's chance to settle in and enjoy all the comforts that home had to offer. Despite such luxuries as a tennis court, a yoga studio, a screening room, a swimming pool with a man-made beach, a guest house, an expansive tiki-bar deck with a thatched roof, and enough streams and ponds to house the world's tadpole population, the house had a very lived-in feel to it. Drew had never been the type to stand on ceremony, and her attitude toward her home was no exception.

"I'm very into cleanliness," Drew explained. "But I'm also not one of those mothers that, like, freaks out if you spill milk. I'm like, 'Cool. Whatever. Let's clean it up.' So my house is very friendly. You can put your feet on anything, and you can enjoy yourself and relax, but you don't sit down and go, 'Eww. There are like fleas and stuff in here.' It's clean enough, but I was always amazed by people's houses when I was younger, [the ones] that were so pristine you felt you couldn't touch anything. I couldn't live like that."

Although in her past relationships, Drew had always been quick to "shack up," her new house was reserved for her and the dogs. To be sure, Luke was still a frequent guest, but despite their best intentions, it was becoming more and more obvious with each passing day that the romance was indeed on its last legs. Albeit far from apocalyptic, the comments they made about their relationship during the November '98 release of *Home Fries* bore little resemblance to the crazy-in-love sentiments that they'd gushed only a year earlier. "Drew and I are lovers, but we need our space," Luke said. Meanwhile, Drew admitted that she and Luke "bicker sometimes, but we never fight."

Despite the good reviews garnered by Luke and Drew's onscreen chemistry, *Home Fries* failed to generate any heat at the box office, bringing in a meager ten million dollars. In an odd bit of cosmic coincidence, the little movie met its dismal fate right around the time that Drew's relationship with Luke was careening toward its own dead end. "You shouldn't put yourself through hell to keep a relationship going," Drew explained. "I'm still fragile. When it comes to love, I have the survivor's instinct to get out before I wind up getting hurt too much or feeling bitter."

Thus, in December of '98, Drew and Luke became a

thing of the past. "I went out with Luke for three great years," she said. "I am so in love with him and it's too bad that we couldn't stick it out longer—not that three years isn't a while. I would like to have had it go on forever. I think you should go into every relationship believing that it has the capacity and potential to do that. I say be a dreamer, believe in it all."

Like all of Drew's romances, this one ended on a very friendly, if bittersweet, note. "Luke and I are really good friends," Drew said, "and we really love each other. I have a greater peace in my relationship [with Luke]." Naturally, Luke was just as willing to remain on good terms with Drew, saying that she's "a wonderful person but it just didn't work out."

While the two stayed mum about the breakup, the split caught the attention of the press when Drew was spotted arm in arm with Jeremy Davies. The thirty-year-old actor, who was best known for his work in *Saving Private Ryan,* had played the town bully to Drew's town Jezebel in *Guncrazy* some seven years earlier. The *New York Post* was the first to legitimize the rumor that the two were dating, but other papers soon followed suit. In a time when she was trying to get over the rupture of a three-year relationship, Drew was in no mood to fend off idle gossip. So, in January, she packed her bags and flew to the lush Hawaiian island of Kauai, by herself.

She'd never taken a vacation alone before, and discovering the many joys of solitude gave Drew a lot to think and smile about. Here she was, a strong and accomplished twenty-four-year-old who could hardly remember the last time she'd been without a man for a stretch longer than a few months. Leland Hayward, Jamie Walters, Jeremy Thomas, Eric Erlandson, Luke Wilson . . . she'd either loved, gotten engaged to, or married them all. Loving herself was the part that had gotten lost in the shuffle. Would that make headlines? Probably not, but Drew was only too happy to stay out of the limelight for the time being.

Her first week on the island, Drew realized how new and exciting being alone could be. After renting a small house by the beach, she hiked through the rainforests, swam in the ocean, and enjoyed looking out at the picturesque views. "Sometimes it's strange," Drew mused, "because I don't have love in my life—in the boyfriend sense. But I have it from other places, and hopefully, always from myself. I no longer have the fear of being alone, because I *am* alone, and it's not scary. It's cool to find out that you don't need a boyfriend to be happy."

Hearing Drew espouse these principles of girl-power would undoubtedly have made her fans very happy. Her tendency to throw herself headlong into every relationship and immerse herself within each successive boyfriend had not been lost on her devoted following, who wished to see Drew loving herself more and trying to be "the perfect girlfriend" less. At last, that breakthrough had arrived. Drew Barrymore was on her own, and for a twenty-four-year-old who'd always been at least ten years ahead of her time, it was none too soon.

Just as Drew had shaken off the post-breakup blues, she was confronted with yet another disappointment. Fox Searchlight Pictures had purchased rights to an independent film called *Boys Don't Cry* at the Sundance Film Festival. The film was about Brandon Teena, the young woman who'd been killed for passing as a male. For the past two years Drew's Flower Films had been working in tandem with Diane Keaton's Blue Relief Productions to bring the story to the big screen. Fox Searchlight's acquisition of *Boys Don't Cry* effectively put the kibosh on Drew's pet project. Not one to hide her feelings, the actress shared the pain of the let down with the world. "I really wanted to do the Brandon Teena movie," Drew admitted. "I wanted to produce and star in it. But, I lost it. I had such a great interest in the film, and told everyone that long before I should have. I have learned to keep my mouth shut."

While the role of Brandon Teena would soon earn Hilary Swank every manner of industry accolade, including an Academy Award and a Golden Globe, Drew was not bitter. Those were the breaks, and she could only applaud the film's producers for having the vision to bring the story to the screen. "More power to them for beating me to it," she said.

Down but not out, Drew quickly turned her attention to other matters. *Never Been Kissed* was due out in April, and she was determined to do everything in her considerable power to make her first producing effort a smashing success. Interviews with magazines were conducted almost around the clock, daytime and late-night talk show appearances were arranged (of course, David Letterman was among the first to be contacted), press junkets were scheduled, and Drew even lucked into her second stint as the host of *Saturday Night Live.*

On second thought, maybe luck didn't have all that much to do with it. Thanks in large part to her casting of *SNL* star Molly Shannon (think Mary Katherine Gallagher of *Superstar* fame) in the role of Josie's wild best friend in *Never Been Kissed,* Drew was an obvious choice for the role of *SNL* host. The fact that she'd already succeeded at hosting the show once before, when she was just seven years old, also didn't hurt. Best of all, the screenwriter behind *The Wedding Singer,* Tim Herlihy, also happened to be the head writer at *SNL.* All things considered, it was a match made in movie-promotion heaven.

Of course, none of this is to say that Drew didn't have her work cut out for her. Poking fun at everyone from Joan Rivers to Gap store employees to Ascot-tie-wearing show-dog-owners was not as easy as Drew made it look. But the ensemble work was nothing compared to the ordeal of concocting a creative opening monologue. The careful reader will recall that Drew's first *SNL* experience saw her scared to death of standing up before a crowd. Back then, she'd chosen to take questions from the audience in lieu of delivering her soliloquy. Seventeen years later, the opening monologue still remained the same, but Drew had changed. She was now ready and raring to go before the madding crowd.

"All I want to do in my monologue is two things," Drew told her friend and *SNL* head writer Tim Herlihy. "I want it to be a musical number 'cause to me those are so funny. And . . . I really wanna make fun of myself, but I don't want it to be so mean that I get a bad taste in my mouth. I don't want it to be so horrible that you walk away going, 'She is an asshole.' "

Sure enough, Drew got exactly what she wanted. Opening the March 14, 1999 *Saturday Night Live* with a song, Drew crooned lyrics that revolved completely around her wild and wacky life story. Refreshing any faded memories, the little ditty rattled off Drew's days as a child star, drug addict, teenage vamp, quickie bride, and *Late Show* flasher. In the span of two minutes, Drew recapped the whole of her life and times and had the audience rolling in the aisles.

A week after her spectacular *SNL* engagement, Drew was once again in the public eye. This time, however, she wasn't promoting a movie, but supporting a friend. For his turn in *American History X,* Edward Norton had been nominated for a Best Actor Oscar and he asked Drew to accompany him to the Academy Awards. Clearly, the two had remained close since costarring in *Everyone Says I Love You,* but many wondered if there wasn't more to this story. Was Drew in love again?

No dice. "No, I am not seeing Edward Norton," Drew insisted. "We are just friends. We were at the Academy Awards together as friends. I am enjoying my singleness."

Drew wasn't kidding about her glee at leading the single life. Although she'd had her ups and downs since breaking up with Luke, on the whole, she had to admit that if the split taught her anything, it was that she'd been coupled for far too long. "Not having a boyfriend,

I'm, like, the happiest I've ever been," she effused. "I travel by myself now, I went to Hawaii by myself. I'm so into romance. I see couples and it's so yummy and beautiful and I can't wait till it happens to me again. And yet I'm excited to be on my own. I'm amazed at how thrilled to bits I am to wake up every day."

Drew had a great many reasons to jump for joy in the spring of '99. First of all, all the publicity that she'd done on behalf of *Never Been Kissed* actually seemed to have paid off. After its April 9 release, the picture scored big at the box office week after week. By the time it was pulled from the theaters, the movie that had cost only fifteen million dollars to make had grossed nearly four times that amount in the U.S. alone. That was a hit in any language.

The newly-minted producer hardly had time to toast her own success before she was up to her elbows in work for her biggest role to date—producing and starring in *Charlie's Angels: The Movie*. For months, Drew had been in talks with Columbia Pictures and Leonard Goldberg, the creator of the original *Charlie's Angels* series, but it was not until April that Drew's top secret project finally got the official go-ahead. Much of the studio's sudden enthusiasm could no doubt be attributed to Drew's tireless behind-the-scenes efforts.

Aside from committing to star in *Charlie's Angels*, Drew had also proven herself as a producer by personally convincing fellow A-list siren Cameron Diaz to costar in the picture. Unlike so many big screen adaptations of popular TV shows, *Charlie's Angels: The Movie* would not revive the original characters of Sabrina Duncan, Kelly Garrett, and Jill Munroe. "These will be entirely different Angels," said producer Leonard Goldberg. "Drew is not playing Sabrina Duncan and Cameron will not be playing Jill Munroe. We are not remaking the series. We're making a big-screen version of it."

Instead, each of the film's three stars would be outfitted with a new identity. Drew would play Dylan, the "tough girl," Diaz would play Natalie, the "bookworm," and Alex, the "class act," would be portrayed by an actress that had yet to be determined.

The fact that Charlie was one Angel shy of a threesome made headlines the world over. Judging by the media's tremendous interest in every detail of the movie's production, millions of people had been waiting for a *Charlie's Angels* film to come along. The media frenzy was unlike anything that Drew had experienced before. The movie was still in the casting phase, and *Entertainment Tonight* and *Access Hollywood* were talking about it already. Talk about pressure; Drew was terrified. She was helping to helm the most anticipated movie of the year, and it was only her second project. What if something went wrong?

"I spent a lot of 1999 being full of fear," Drew admitted. "Everything, I thought, could physically hurt me, whether it was a flight of steps or being on an airplane. I was just very scared. I wasn't doing any characters. I was just sort of producing this movie the whole time and being in the office . . . and I just found myself so scared."

This fear for her own safety must have been an outgrowth of Drew's many film-related anxieties. Take, just for instance, all the hoopla that went into finding an actress to play Alex. From day one, the entertainment press made an artform out of speculating on who would wind up in the movie. Angelina Jolie, Jada Pinkett, Catherine Zeta-Jones, Thandie Newton, Liv Tyler, Lauryn Hill, and Penelope Cruz were just a few of the rumored contenders. Believe it or not, even a couple of Spice Girls were implicated in the gossip pages.

Neither was Drew the only one of the film's producers to be blown away by the media circus. Even Leonard Goldberg, a man many believed had seen and heard it all, was taken aback, if not downright frightened, by the unrelenting gossip. "We never approached Posh Spice, just as we never approached Ginger Spice," he maintained. "It's scary how this movie has taken on a life of its own . . . We have a list of possible third Angels and we are narrowing down that list until we are all settled on one person and then we'll bring the offer to her. . . . We have never issued a single press release on this movie, but each week I pick up the trade papers and see an article claiming we're in negotiations with a new actress. It's not true."

Of course, some of the rumors were true. Angelina Jolie and Jada Pinkett had both been on the short list to play Alex. Much to Drew's consternation, however, both women had passed on the role. Jada Pinkett chose to pursue another role, saying, "I think I'm going to do Spike [Lee]'s next movie." Meanwhile, Angelina Jolie attributed her ambivalence to modesty: "I'm not at that point in my career," she said, "so audiences won't have as much fun watching me run around in high heels chasing bad guys and flipping my hair."

Clearly, securing a third Angel wasn't as easy as it seemed. In fact, in October '99, Drew and the rest of the *Angels* team thought they'd found their Alex in Thandie Newton of *Beloved* and *Mission: Impossible 2* fame when negotiations fell through. With the whole world watching, and filming set to start on December 6, the fiasco was a producer's worst nightmare.

Panic-stricken, the producers and casting directors shifted into high gear to find the third Angel. Then, just a few weeks before cameras began to roll, *Ally McBeal*'s Lucy Liu signed on to play Alex. At last, Drew, along with the rest of the *Charlie's Angel*-loving world, could breathe a deep sigh of relief.

When one considers all the consternation that went into finalizing the *Charlie's Angels* screenplay and the arduous process of casting Bill Murray in the role of the Angels' sidekick Bosley, it's no wonder that Drew's fear of failure had escalated into a sort of hypochondria. But now that all systems were go, Drew's outlook brightened considerably. "Now that we're [filming]," she said, "I feel so liberated and it's so exciting."

Spending December '99 and much of the year 2000 at work on *Charlie's Angels*, Drew also made room in her daily planner to voice the role of Piolet in *Titan A.E.*, an animated, science fiction film that also starred Matt Damon and Bill Pullman. With both films scheduled for summer 2000 release dates, audiences would have gotten a double dose of Drew had the release of

Charlie's Angels not been pushed back to November 2000.

The new release date was inevitable considering the casting difficulties that *Angels* encountered in 1999. While summer pics traditionally fare better than those released in the fall, Drew was confident that the movie could succeed on its own merits. "What I love about it is it's girls getting to do what boys do," she said about the movie. "Not girls being men, but girls being feminine and doing what men do."

By all accounts, the filming of the movie itself went off without a hitch. Drew, who was being paid nine million dollars to star and coproduce, found herself having a wonderful time laughing at Bill Murray's jokes and bonding with her female costars. Although the hype for the movie never let down for so much as a moment, Drew was no longer worried. From where she was standing, *Charlie's Angels* and her career were going to be just fine.

In 1999, *Entertainment Weekly* had ranked Drew as the ninety-first most powerful person in all of Entertainment. Of the actresses who made *EW*'s "Power 101" list, Drew ranked fifth, second only to Julia Roberts and Oscar-winners Jodie Foster, Helen Hunt, and Gwyneth Paltrow. Hollywood had finally acknowledged Drew's clout, both as a producer and as an actress, but the twenty-four-year-old at the midst of all these accolades was far too busy to pay any mind to lip service. She'd worked all her life to get to the top, and there was no reason to stop now.

Drew serves as an example for anyone who believes that there's no way to climb the ladder without stepping on a few toes. At every point in her career, she's elicited nothing but raves from her coworkers. Thanks to her easygoing manner and light-hearted attitude, making friends such as Adam Sandler, who gifted her with a jukebox on her twenty-fourth birthday, and Edward Norton, whom she accompanied to the Academy Awards, has come naturally to Drew.

Although her early years as a hard core party-tot are now the province of Hollywood Babylon, her family problems have not disappeared. She is still not on speaking terms with her mother, who decided that writing a tell-all book and putting Drew's baby clothes and personal belongings up on the Internet auction block would somehow bring them closer together. She's also accepted her father's wayward ways and, unable to change him or help him, made peace with the fact that, like it or not, these are her parents, for better or for worse.

If Drew's family life has been rife with tears and disappointment, her social and work spheres are replete with satisfaction and good cheer. She knows exactly how far she's come, who her friends are, and where she's headed. As she told one reporter, "I feel my career is like an ocean current right now. I'll continue to be employed. I won't be just a big splash."

Last, while Drew may not be in a romantic relationship right now, she has finally found the greatest love of all, the kind of love everlasting that will keep her happy, healthy, and bursting at the seams with positive energy for the rest of her days. "My whole life I have hoped that I would find someone . . . who would make me feel like they weren't going to leave," she expressed. "I've finally found someone who does that for me. And it's so exciting because it's *me*. It's the weirdest revelation I've ever had. I will always be there for myself. . . ."

Acknowledgments

A world of thanks to Cathy Repetti, our hardworking editor, who gave us the opportunity to pursue this book. As always, we thank Giles Anderson, our wonderful agent, for all his efforts on our behalf. Thanks also to our mom for her invaluable support and exceptional research skills, as well as to John Nikkah, who never fails to cheer us up.

Last but most definitely not least, we have to thank all the newspapers, magazines, TV shows, and websites that have made it their business to work the Barrymore beat. This book would not have been possible without the following sources: America Online, the *Calgary Sun*, the *Chicago Sun-Times*, *The Columbian*, *Cosmopolitan*, *The Dallas Morning News*, *Details*, *E! Online*, *ET Online*, *E! True Hollywood Story*, *Entertainment Tonight*, *Entertainment Weekly*, *GQ*, *Harper's Bazaar*, *Hollywood Online*, *In Style*, *Interview*, *Jane*, *This Evening with Judith Regan*, *London Free Press*, *Los Angeles Times*, *Mademoiselle*, *Marie Claire*, *Mr. Showbiz*, *Newsday*, *Oprah*, *The Orange County Register*, *Ottawa Sun*, *Parade Magazine*, *People*, *People Online*, *The Record* (Bergen County, New Jersey), *Seventeen*, *Star Interviews* by Prairie Miller, *Sugar* magazine, *Teen*, *Teen People*, *Time*, *Toronto Star*, *Toronto Sun*, *Total Film*, *University Wire*, *US Magazine*, *USA Today*, *USA Weekend*, *Well Rounded Entertainment*, *WI Light Online*, *Young & Modern*.

Leah and Elina Furman are New York–based writers, and sisters, who have coauthored many books, including *In His Eyes: The Julio Iglesias Jr. Story, Rock Your World: Meet the Moffatts, The Heat Is On: 98°, Heart of Soul: The Lauryn Hill Story, Felicity: Meet the Stars, James Van Der Beek,* and *The Everything After College Book.*

Printed in the United States
by Baker & Taylor Publisher Services